From Gravel to Glory

Becoming a House of God

Gina Calvert

From Gravel to Glory: Becoming a House of God
© 2008 by DeWard Publishing Company, Ltd.
P.O. Box 6259, Chillicothe, Ohio 45601
800.300.9778
www.dewardpublishing.com

Cover design and brick wall graphics by Katrina Calvert.

Reasonable care has been taken to trace original sources for any excerpts and quotations appearing in this book and to document such information in the footnotes. For material not the public domain, fair-use standards and practices were followed. Should any attribution be found to be incorrect or incomplete, the publisher welcomes written documentation supporting correction for subsequent printings.

Printed in the United States of America.

ISBN: 978-0-9798893-5-6

While God waits for His temple to be built of love,
men bring stones.

Rabindranath Tagore

Foreword

Does it seem like you are living your life from one crisis to the next? Do you struggle to make sense of the hardships and suffering you and your loved ones experience? Do you find it puzzling to understand how others can "consider it all joy" when facing trials of many kinds (Jas 1.2)?

With a brilliant use of metaphor, *From Gravel to Glory* offers understanding to those who love God but struggle to make sense of the events of life. A gifted communicator, Gina Calvert utilizes authentic life examples to share the "bigger picture" of the Christian experience. As a result, readers can use the examples and metaphors of reconstruction to make sense of the seeming setbacks and detours of life. Gina shares depth and meaning, offering hope as she brings significance to the ordinary.

From Gravel to Glory contains a timeless message that continues to offer new understanding reading after reading. The book will become part of my reserve collection of those books which I keep and reread every few years.

Julie P. Combs, Ed.D.
Professor and Educational Consultant
Author: *Managing Conflict: 50 Strategies for Leaders*

Preface

Many years in ministry have taught me that it is through our stories that we help each other hold on. It took me a while to learn that presenting a perfect image of myself did not encourage others in their spiritual journey. As God drew me deeper into ministry, I found that the people around me were most helped when I revealed the secrets which rebelled most vehemently against being told. I learned from author and actress Nicole Johnson that extending my "withered hand" in complete disclosure resulted in healing where secrecy did not, and holding out my healed-but-scarred hand—as Jesus did to the skeptical Thomas—proved His presence to others better than all my words. I consider this treatise to be the extension of both the withered and the healed-but-scarred parts of me.

As I show my scars and the path to healing that I continue to travel, it is necessary that I also share my wounds—though I do so with hesitation. My desire is to reveal Jesus as I have experienced Him through these wounds, not to accuse others or to elicit sympathy for myself.

Nor do I seek admiration. I am not a Bible scholar and am well aware that my reflections touch only the edges of a reality none of us can really know as we are hampered by what Carl Jung called "the poverty of language."[1] So I have tried to simply recount the conversation I have had with God through His Word and the developing relationship with Him through two decades of confusion and pain. My turmoil was not more noteworthy—and especially not more sensational—than others' stories, but my ability to avoid many of the pitfalls of the teen years, and my marriage to a preacher at the age of nineteen, left me feeling in control of the life I planned to spend in service to God and shocked when it didn't turn out the way I had planned. In reality, I didn't even start my part of this conversation with God until that life crashed into a wall built of my own ignorance and stubbornness.

Recognizing myself to be a "ragamuffin"—author Brennan Manning's word for a person who is "bent and bruised, and feels that their life is a grave disappointment to God"[2]—initiated the turnaround in my journey that brought me face to face with Him. I have found myself being used by God far more from the condition of being patched up than He ever could or did when I thought I had it all together.

If you are a person confused about how to harmonize your struggles, sin or sorrow with your spiritual journey and the promises of God, this book is for you. It is my prayer that you will find within your current circumstances, and within these pages, the recognition of Jesus, the stimulus of the Spirit, and the love of the Father.

With Deep Gratitude

for **the Holy Ones**, who wooed me, healed me, and taught me everything I know.

for my husband **Steve**, my first role model in thinking outside my little box. He walked every inch of this exploration with me in experience, relived them through many, many hours of conversation, and cooked his own dinner a few times during the writing. His support and love have given me both roots and wings. I love you, Steve!

for my children **Katrina, Danica** and **Jared**, who have not only taught me much, but also have put up with me in all the stages before Jesus began to change me… and since. Parenting them has helped me understand so much about God and the good intentions He has toward me. I'm so grateful to Katrina for designing my cover.

for **Charlie Jarvis**, a stranger who approached me on an airplane and confirmed God's message that I was to write a book, then became my first reader and editor, and my friend. This book would not exist without his unfailing support through the insecurity and doubt of the first draft, and his absolute trust in what God was trying to do through me.

for **Peni Jean Rutter**, whose editorial input came when it was time for the book—and me!—to grow up. Peni pushed me to dig deeper, write better and laugh harder than I knew how to on my own.

for my parents **Glenn and Anna Burt,** for the foundation of biblical studies they provided for me, as well as the unwavering faith and love for God they have modeled to me throughout my entire life.

for my friends **Julie Combs, Ethan Laurence, Chris Harrison, Justin Chetelat, Deondra Selph, Janice Ingram, Robyn Knight** and my sisters **Donna Myers** and **Glenda Cheek,** all of whom let me do my thinking out loud. Your contributions are woven throughout the book... and not just in the personal stories you allowed me to use about you! I am grateful for the technical assistance of **Ryan Hochdorf** and **Brynlea Taylor,** and the encouragement of the believers at **The Branch,** who reminded me that "with God, nothing shall be impossible!"

Contents

Open Your Eyes: Seeing the House Plans

Making Sense Out of Change 13

Transformation: A Primal Reality 25

Sanctuary: The Blueprints of Transformation 35

Clean Sweep: Keep, Toss or Sell 49

Falling Apart: Between Invitation and Healing 59

Men Bring Stones 81

Open Your Mind: Participating in the Building Process

Do-It-Yourself Detective Kit 103

Defining Moments 125

Open Your Heart: Enjoying the House

Total Perspective Vortex: You are Here 149

Epilogue: The Face of the Father 167

Open Your Eyes

Seeing the House Plans

*It has seemed to me sometimes as though the Lord breathes on this
poor gray ember of Creation and it turns to radiance—for a moment or a
year or the span of a life. And then it sinks back into itself again, and to look
at it no one would know it had anything to do with fire, or light. ...But the
Lord is more constant and far more extravagant than it seems to imply.
Wherever you turn your eyes, the world can shine like transfiguration.
You don't have to bring a thing to it except a little willingness to see.
Only, who could have the courage to see it?*

Marilynne Robinson, *Gilead*[1]

1

Making Sense Out of Change

"If you're not confused, you're not paying attention."

Tom Peters

My friend Kevin recently told me about an odd conversation his sister had with a coworker that went something like this:

"Do you have any sense?" she asked.

"Well... I *think* I do," he replied, wondering where this was leading.

"What do you mean, you *think* you do? Would you check?"

"Uhhh"—long pause—"I'm pretty sure I do."

"Okaaay."—her irritation mounting—"So will you see how much you have?"

"Ummm"—his confusion increasing—"Exactly how do you want me to do that?"

"Well," she said in a stinging tone, "For starters, you could look in your *pocket.*"

Ah. Now he got it. Contemplating and measuring his common sense would have been unnecessary if he had been able to *read* his colleague's words: "Do you have any cents?" And Kevin's sister's frustration might have been lessened if she had been aware that her word for "change" was being completely misunderstood.

You've probably experienced similar misunderstandings. Conversations—and lives—are frequently affected by this kind of perplexity as we attempt to make "cents" not only of "change" but of pain, sin, and all the challenges we face. In the midst of our struggles, we can be convinced that our perceptions and conclusions are perfectly logical, yet feel baffled by the ensuing misunderstanding and lack of resolution to our difficulties. And this confusion has a way of escalating into even more bewilderment because of our natural reaction to pain and trouble: resistance.

I perfected resistance early on. As a young child, I hated going to the doctor to get shots. No child enjoys shots, but I was so opposed to this process that during one doctor visit before I started school, I tensed up so tightly while receiving a shot in the backside that the needle actually broke off in my muscle tissue!

If physical pain is all that is involved, resolution will come as soon as the pain subsides, but we have an innate tendency to attach meaning to our pain which becomes intertwined with our emotional DNA. Perhaps you have seen the look in the eye of a child being restrained by his mother in order to receive an injection. In addition to the fear of the sharp, pointy object that is being jabbed into his little thigh—and the pain it causes—he is clearly puzzled. Within those liquid eyes, questions form wordlessly in rapid succession with remarkable clarity: "What's happening to me?" "Why is this happening to me?" "Why is my mother not helping me?" "Wait a minute, my mother is a part of this!" Thus begins his struggle to make sense of the origins of pain and what it means to him.

Like all children, I objected to pain and discomfort, but long after the physical distress had abated, I continued to be mystified and saddened that my pain had come from the very ones I expected to protect me from those things. I didn't have the faculties to grasp why my mother would deliberately allow me to suffer. I took this to a higher level than most children; I suffered from chronic depression before most people had ever even heard of it.

I continued to wrestle with this confusion as I grew older and experienced similar conflict between my concept of God's love and my unsubstantiated beliefs about what His love was supposed to look and feel like. My uncertainty resulted in blindness to any

painful and uncomfortable truths about myself and my relationship with God, which prevented me from trusting Him and receiving healing at points in my life during times of physical and
spiritual exhaustion. I paid lip service to the idea of trusting that
God knew what was best for me, but in reality I was angry, hurt,
miserable and resentful about the struggles I was experiencing in
my day to day life.

It was not until I held my own resistant daughter down for her
shots that I began to connect the dots about God allowing pain
for the purposes of growth, but it was a slow realization. For a
long time, if the source was unexpected, or the cause unantici-
pated or undeserved, or if I didn't see the immediate purpose, I
could not connect it to God in any kind of constructive way.

It was particularly difficult when it occurred in the arena of
spirituality. Because of the struggles my husband and I faced, we
began a quest for deeper spiritual understanding, but our questions and changes in our doctrinal belief system elicited accusations from fellow Christians of being divisive and seeking to sub-
vert the church. We were not prepared for the confusing physical
and emotional ramifications of these charges. We parted ways
with four different church families over a stretch of twelve years
under stressful circumstances as our journey became increasingly
upsetting to, and less compatible with, the needs and expectations
of those churches. Because my husband Steve was working with
these churches in a position of ministry, these moves caused severe
upheaval in our family. The inherent stress in processing painful
conflict and rejection, moving several states away, repeatedly up-
rooting our family, juggling our limited financial resources, and
trying to hold our marriage together with duct tape and prayer
took a severe toll on our emotional and spiritual health.

Existing in a perpetual state of crisis for such an extended period of time crystallized my awareness of a strange phenomenon
which exists in me—and which I have observed in many other
people. Most people agree with the idea that life is a struggle,
that difficult things are going to happen to us and that they serve
a purpose. And yet, as I said earlier, our most common reaction to

struggles is resistance, discouragement and confusion. Even those with a spiritual outlook often feel that life is slamming them into brick walls, presenting them with a completely random set of circumstances, or balancing precariously on luck. This dichotomy (life is hard/why is my life so hard?) reveals an innate belief that we should not have to struggle.

Emerson said, "The sun shines and warms and lights us and we have no curiosity to know why this is so; but we ask the reason of all evil, of pain, and hunger, and mosquitoes and silly people." Deep down we have an expectation that reality, as long as it is good, is just as it should be, but if it is unpleasant or unjust, something is wrong. This presents a dilemma. Someone must be held accountable! A lot of people seem to start by blaming God—even atheists. It is always interesting to meet individuals who claim not to believe in God but are angry with Him. It seems safe to say that sometimes atheism is really only a response to—or resistance against—disappointment in the Originator and Sustainer of the order of things. It can be a way of minimizing the impact of pain when we can't seem to find or accept its purpose.

For some people, resistance comes in the form of believing that God does exist and that He is sadistically torturing them. I saw this once in my sixteen-year old daughter during a difficult relocation from one city to another. She was sitting in the front seat of our car, holding her turtle in a plastic bin in her lap. There was just a little water in there and she noticed that as the movement of the car tipped the bin back and forth, he would scramble to keep from sliding, but he always slid anyway. For awhile, she exaggerated the bin-tipping, fascinated with the turtle's efforts, and then she said, "This is what God is doing to me."

Others resist by interpreting struggles as God's deafness or indifference. Some of the most difficult blows to my faith have been delivered by what I perceived to be the silence of God. Difficult circumstances which persist despite fervent prayer and earnest obedience challenge our faith like nothing else. Surprisingly, even those who rarely give God a backward glance have the expectation that He should cushion their path. Their struggles become proof that God is not to be trusted. Their criteria for determining if God exists, if He is a loving God and if He really answers prayers, are based solely on whether or not they are getting all that they want.

This belief that God is responsible for all our struggles actually reveals a fantastic faith that there is a Being who is capable of managing everything and that if such a Being existed, it would be a good Being (as we define good). This faith falls short, however, when we begin to experience circumstances we define as bad. Distrust that goodness or love governs the execution of our circumstances is at the root of much of our pain.

One of the most common forms of resistance is our tendency to blame other people for our difficulties (while simultaneously blaming God *for* those people). It's true that people can be shallow and self-absorbed, cruel and hurtful—and that's just our friends and family. They will break our hearts and make our lives difficult. So we break up, move out, pull away, retaliate or reject, then start all over with new people, never realizing that the common denominator in all our relationship struggles is *us*, or that the challenges of relationships have value far beyond the visible elements on which we fixate.

I'm not just talking about unbelievers. These are also the reactions of Christians, individuals who truly long to be better people. We want to grow, to achieve the transformation we expected when first we met God, to be freed from our sin, our addictions and our fickle bouts of determination. The problem comes when this righteous desire is infiltrated by our misinformed conclusions about what God and the people in our lives are doing in relation to us. These misunderstandings are like tenacious vines creeping across the surface of a wall, obscuring the truth about how God is working in us. We mistakenly believe that the hidden surface—our spiritual growth—hinges on three things: How God and others are cooperating, experiencing our definition of a manageable amount of trouble and setbacks in our life, and the consistency of our own effort. So we desire. We try hard. And when nothing seems to change, we blame God or others.

Extreme Makeovers

Before we can see the underlying structure of our spiritual growth, we must pull away the stubborn vine, examining first the significance and inherent integrity—but also misconceptions—of our longing to improve. The desire to be better than we are is reflected in the current obsession with makeovers, which permeate television and magazines. It began with "spaces," the trendy word for rooms. It wasn't long before the alterations went *extreme*, surgically producing dramatic physical transformations. Makeover mania now includes entire houses, landscapes, wardrobes, weight loss, relationships, and disorganized families with unruly children. While the shows can be engaging and entertaining, I find it more interesting to observe the skyrocketing popularity of the idea that total transformations can occur in an hour, including commercials.

Our interest in extreme makeovers is not merely a reflection of our fondness for perfection, but an innate connection to the process of transformation. By observing the method by which others are changed, we find hope for our own reformation. The attraction to stories is a central theme in Donald Miller's *Blue Like Jazz*.[3] He explains that elements exist in stories because they exist in reality. The classic elements we see in literature—setting, conflict, climax and resolution—exist because we experience those things in real life. This means that although our efforts are often misdirected, we connect to stories of transformation because we want to be transformed, and because, at any given moment, we are *involved* in several stories of transformation, each with a setting, a conflict, a climax (what Miller calls a point of decision) and a resolution.

I remember learning this truth about stories when I was young. I was very opposed to the idea that a good story needed conflict to be interesting and relevant to the reader. Even back then, I wanted not only happy endings, but happy beginnings and middles too! My difficulty in understanding the relevance of my struggles stemmed from experiencing the story elements of my life in isolation from each other, in failing to recognize the relationship between those elements. If I saw my daily commute in traffic as merely a setting for a particular chapter in my life (perhaps entitled How I Learned that the World Does Not Revolve Around Me), and not simply one more proof on my list of why God hates me, I would view the conflict in that story differently and watch for the climactic moment that will resolve that chapter. I would become more of a conscious participant, and not view myself simply a helpless, hapless puppet.

Consider

Aristotle coined the phrase *first philosophy* to describe the need to persistently seek the original cause and ultimate principle behind each proven reality, to dig deeper beneath each layer of scientific discovery. This makes sense for us, as well. If stories of transformation reflect elements of reality, then we are led to the author of transformation—God—for greater insights into the nature of transformation.

One of God's favorite themes is that of maturing, developing and growing. He draws on the universally understood experience of being born and growing up with all the qualities and developmental stages inherent in being human. This is also reflected in nature—seeds, soil quality, roots, fruits and vines are all true mirrors to those who are acquainted with that world, whether it be an expert gardener, a tourist in a redwood forest, or a child discovering bees and the wonders of cross-pollination. These processes do not occur so repeatedly throughout our world simply for the sake of producing food or human adults or to keep us from getting bored with one season. Their persistently recurring nature tells me that God is using these natural elements to awaken us to spiritual realities.

In addition to the natural world, God's work on us is likened to the process of being refined by fire to help us see how our trials bring our impurities to the surface for removal. There's also His clay analogy: we're a lump of clay being molded and fired into a container meant to be beautiful and durable, but more importantly, to contain something. He also says we are a temple of the Living God.[4] All these images teach us that we are hardwired to become something different, something better, and they serve to connect our daily lives with our spiritual journey, to give us a deeper and broader perspective to view our experiences with.

You knew that. I think I must have too. Yet when it came to the need for practical help in my daily life, seeking God had begun to feel like running through a maze and finding only dead ends, with no escape and no guidance. Eventually, I began to see that God has hidden secrets in these word pictures, mysteries for us to discover through close attention. "Consider the lilies," Jesus said. [5] Perhaps it was time to ponder His creations like a detective, to develop a curiosity about why He chose to craft the delicate frames of orchids with such masterful detail, to listen with a quiet heart to the subtle insights revealed in the whirring conversation of insects. Maybe I should look deeper at predictable patterns in relationships or human behavior for a God-perspective that was surely hidden there. What had I missed by rushing through life, distracted by man's inventions, and oblivious to God's efforts to reach my mind and my heart through every aspect of His word and His creation? While I shouted, "Why?" His whispered, incarnate answers went unheard.

The *why?* I was asking was satisfied unexpectedly one day when a picture God had been painting for me for several years was suddenly completed. It was a blueprint of His Holy Temple, a symbol which is rarely presented as a metaphor for growth or transformation. Because I knew very little about temples—just as I knew little about plants, pottery and gold-refining—much of God's word picture, or explanation, had been lost on me. Suddenly, the metaphor of a temple created a meaningful context for my struggles; it linked my difficulties, mostly unrecognized for what they were, with love.

Part of the reason we miss the significance of the temple is because we are single-minded about buildings. Unless we are in the construction industry, when most of us imagine our dream home, we see its appearance, the gadgets and features our friends will envy, the way we would furnish it, and the way we would live in it. It is unlikely that these fantasies include R-factors in insulation or details about electricity, heating and air conditioning, but when things go wrong, the most beautiful house in the world can toggle-switch your brain to a deep interest in plumbing, shifting foundations or black mold. Try to hang a door and suddenly you're going to care about un-square construction. Pay your electric bill and discover an unknown affection for attic ventilation and BTUs. Trouble directs our attention from the appearance to the construction.

Although it would be less painful and arduous if we could separate the building *process* from the actual finished *building*, it is in that very process where the beauty and calamity of our lives unite with the reality of being a holy temple. Being a temple of God, it turns out, is at the heart of our relationship with Him. Until we see how that temple is built, we will miss the eternal significance of the ordinary, the stubborn, the excruciating, and maybe even the triumphant moments of our lives. And we will miss the love that builds.

Oh, we will give God the credit for the good things—*"God-things,"* as people like to call them these days—those times when He serendipitously brings people into our lives to comfort and teach us, when things are going extraordinarily well, when we're experiencing intimacy with Him and our prayers are being answered just as we would like. But until we understand His building techniques, we will miss that it's *all* a God-thing: the agonizing silence between jobs; the periods of infertility that may or may not end in pregnancy; the struggle to stay married; the incessant clamor of our flesh; the times of isolation and loneliness; the spiritual deserts; the silly people; even the moral failures.

To say that everything is a God-thing is not to blame God for our troubles. Many of our experiences are, directly or indirectly, the consequences of our own choices. Many are the consequences of other peoples' choices. Many are just the reality of living in a fallen and temporary world, of being affected by time and chance, which happen to [us] all.[6] But here is what I know for sure: God has designed all of life—everything that happens and everything we feel—as tools for the transformation He is working in each of us. I believe this without reservation because He has said that "all things work together for good to those who love the Lord." [7]

By asserting this to be true, God declares victory over everything: all that we do to ourselves, all that others do to us, all that life puts us through, and especially all that Satan intends for evil. You may think you know this, especially in hindsight, or you may strongly disagree. Maybe this will become a convenient excuse for retaining God as a scapegoat for your problems, or you might just want to curl up into the fetal position at the news that God is behind some of your discomfort. I invite you to keep an open mind as we examine all the facets of this claim. Scripture is clear on this. The challenge is developing the ability to *see* and *rest* in the fact that everything you experience—everything in *this* moment—is *ultimately* a God-thing, and that every God-thing works together for your good in your life right now, always motivated by His love for you.

This is my journey, my understanding of how I am becoming something new and discovering a better way to meet the challenges that come into my life. Through the metaphor of the temple, the transformation process has become surprisingly constant, recognizable and comforting for me, and my love for Jesus Christ and my faith and trust in God have rocketed far beyond what I could have achieved through my own effort.

Don't get me wrong; there has been enormous effort on my part—some of it effective, some of it not so much. You should know up front that I'm not offering any easy answers or shortcuts. Understanding this process won't keep you from struggling with personal issues or experiencing pain. On the contrary, I'm *challenging* you to struggle, but with a different perspective, to work smarter not harder. I want you to stretch your boundaries and your willingness to endure discomfort, not so you can transform yourself, but so you can get yourself out of the way of what God is doing to transform you.

The connection between discomfort and transformation is

cleverly expressed in Fiona Apple's song *Extraordinary Machine*,[8] which states that the consequence of avoiding discomfort is that we stay the same:

> I still only travel by foot, and by foot, its a slow climb,
> But I'm good at being uncomfortable, so
> I can't stop changing all the time.
>
> I notice that my opponent is always on the go
> And won't go slow, so's not to focus, and I notice
> He'll hitch a ride with any guide, as long as
> They go fast from whence he came
> But he's no good at being uncomfortable, so
> He can't stop staying exactly the same.

What does it look like to be "good at being uncomfortable"? It isn't necessarily the absence of turmoil or complaint, but rather a willingness to reevaluate the meanings we have attached to our struggles. When we stop viewing all things in isolation from one another and begin to connect our faith in God's eternal purposes to the tiniest details of our daily lives, we will begin to see our transformations. As our focus shifts from *why* this is happening to *Who* is guiding the process, anger and despair will dissipate into the clarity and peace that is the natural result of trusting God to do a better job of running our lives than we can.

2

Transformation
A Primal Reality

"You know what's weird? Everything is exactly the same and then all of a sudden, everything's different."

Bill Watterson, *Calvin and Hobbes*

My husband and I once bought a dilapidated, roachy house in San Antonio, Texas and turned it into an adorable Mary Engelbreit cottage. We spent about $6,000 redoing every surface, and two years later, we sold the house for a $25,000 profit. In our home renovation, we addressed *surfaces,* we changed the *appearance* of the house, but we made no structural alterations. The house was roach-free, brighter, and cuter, but the bathrooms remained too small, the kitchen floor continued to slant a little, and the doors occasionally still stuck when the weather was humid. It *looked* transformed, but structurally, it was the same house.

Before I discovered how transformation happens, I thought it was simply an improvement. It's important to know that transformation is more than just an upgrade. It is the difference between a caterpillar and a butterfly, a complete do-over, starting with one thing and ending with another. Author and psychologist Wayne Dyer says, "Literally speaking, transformation is *to go beyond your form.*"

In a world where natural law dictates the decline of everything, transformation is quite miraculous. When we consider the notion of changing a *form*, especially a spiritual one, it is difficult to imagine being able to produce this change ourselves. A biblical perspective confirms this difficulty. In 2 Corinthians 3.18, we find that "We all, with unveiled face, beholding as in a mirror the glory of the Lord, are being transformed into the same image from glory to glory, just as by the Spirit of the Lord."

The fact is, it is not simply difficult. The goal of our transformation is impossible for us: *The image of the glory of the Lord!* We're not just being transformed into better people or even Christ-like people. Attempting to be Christ-like is the equivalent of working on what we can see in ourselves: the surface—which is a good starting point. No matter how hard we try, we can't make ourselves into the same image of glory we see in Christ. We can't go beyond our own form; we will always still be us, even if we manage to improve ourselves somewhat. This is because we are working from the outside in, but His work is concentrated on the foundations and internal structures of who we are. Jesus transforms us from the inside out, beginning in places we can't even see. If we are able to transform ourselves, why would we need God?

Giving Credit Where Credit is Due

Whenever Scripture refers to God transforming us it is stated as an action that is being done *to* us, not *by* us. We *are being* transformed. For a while, I misunderstood passages such as Romans 12.1–2:

> I urge you therefore, brethren, by the mercies of God, to present your bodies a living and holy sacrifice, acceptable to God, which is your spiritual service of worship. And do not be conformed to this world, but be transformed by the renewing of your mind, that you may prove what the will of God is, that which is good and acceptable and perfect. (NASB)

This scripture contrasts two different changes of form: "be not conformed (together-formed) to the world, but be transformed (beyond-formed) by the renewing of your mind." For a long time, it seemed to me that if I could just renew my mind, I could avoid conforming to the world, and transform myself. Both the mind-renewal and the transformation were my job.

I had it all wrong. If you study the passage above, you will see in the first sentence that my spiritual service of worship is to present my body as a living sacrifice. In the second sentence, the verbs *be conformed* and *be transformed* are passive; they signify the difference between moving and being moved, leading and being led. One is from our own power, the other is not. And if we are not *being* transformed, we are *being* conformed, whether or not that is our intent.

The phraseology of my task is direct: "present yourself." This is something I must do. For many years I tried to be a good Christian by attempting—unsuccessfully—to renew my own mind. When I contrasted that failure with the amazing transformative changes I experienced when I presented my body as a living sacrifice, I learned that the renewing of my mind is part of the package.

But let's say for the sake of argument that I *could* manage renewal of my mind. How the miracle of becoming something different grows out of that is most certainly outside the scope of my capabilities. It would be like assuming food is the cause of growth of the body. I have known of small children who eat healthily, but do not grow, perhaps because of disease, hormone imbalance or the inability to absorb nutrients. The complex interplay of nutrition and physiological systems teaches me that while we must eat to grow, growing is not something we control. Cause and effect is not always the simple matter we believe it to be, especially when it comes to spiritual matters.

My experience is living proof that I am not capable of "proving the good, acceptable and perfect will of God,"[1] but when I offer myself as a living sacrifice, He renews my mind toward His thinking, which lessens my tendency to conform to the world's thinking. The new form I become is the ultimate proof of His perfect will.

In his excellent book *Invitation to a Journey*, Robert Mulholland contrasts the idea of *being transformed* with the Christian tendency to *do* as a way of living out our spiritual formation. He does not say that we don't have things to do, but that the things we do are merely the vehicle, not the agent of change:

> We fail to realize that the process of spiritual shaping is a primal reality of human existence. Everyone is in a process of spiritual formation! Every thought we hold, every decision we make, every action we take, every emotion we allow to shape our behavior, every response we make to the world around us, every relationship we enter into, every reaction we have toward the things that surround us and impinge upon our lives—all of these things, little by little, are shaping us into some kind of being.[2]

Perhaps you've worked long and hard in your efforts to change or to be found pleasing to God. Perhaps you've struggled with one or more specific issues for so long that you doubt transformation is occurring in you. I certainly had reason to feel that way with the issues in my life. Struggles in the realms of sexuality, infertility, church problems that included false allegations, depression and dependency on God-substitutes have permeated throughout the better part of 29 years, even as I was actively serving God. It has taken me awhile to understand that these things I have named are not the real issues. They are the cracks in the wall created by an unstable foundation. God doesn't want to just plaster those cracks, paint over them and call them good as new. He wants to fix the foundation: the pride, the fear, the selfishness, the heartaches, the unbelief.

Do you see the difference? I had been trying to transform my *issues*, while He was interested in transforming *me*. There is a place for my efforts, as we'll discuss in the second half of the book, but my guess is you've been trying this for quite a while and have found it to be quite discouraging. Once you see what God is doing, you can go about your part without worrying about the end result, "being confident of this very thing, that He who has begun a good work in you will complete it until the day of Jesus Christ."[3]

Why We Don't See

One of our greatest challenges is learning to perceive physical and spiritual things with spiritual eyes. We discussed earlier that the truths about our spiritual lives are often hidden by misconceptions we have about them, but often we do not recognize transformation in progress because, unlike television makeovers, ours are not accomplished in an hour. We view our progress the way we view the glacial pace of growth in our children, who are the same size until one day they're suddenly not. In actuality, they were growing imperceptibly all along. While they experience growth spurts where change is more visible—and spiritually, we do too—these might be likened to periods of sprinting in a marathon.

Kevin Klein's character in the movie *Life as a House*[4] observed, "Sometimes change can be so constant you don't even feel a difference until there is one. It can be so slow that you don't even know that your life is better or worse until it is. Or it can just blow you away and make you something different in an instant." The apostle Paul's awareness that "though outwardly we are wasting away, yet inwardly we are being renewed day by day,"[5] lends credence to the idea that even in those moments when our lives seem changed in an instant, we are simply experiencing the tipping point of progress that has been occurring internally by the working of the Spirit in our lives.

The reality of unrealized change is exacerbated by the fact that we, like those slow-growing children, are not always cooperative. Fortunately, our stubbornness does not deter God—He is patient in His efforts to transform—but it definitely hinders, prolongs, and intensifies our process.

Second, long projects almost always reach plateaus where we become discouraged by slow progress and start to focus on all that is left to do rather than all that has been accomplished. If you've ever dieted, you know what I mean! From our internal-but-limited perspective, we feel like the people rebuilding Jerusalem's wall under Nehemiah's leadership: "The strength of the laborers is failing and there is so much rubbish that we are not able to build the wall."[6]

Interestingly, the people had already built the wall up to half its height in a short amount of time despite difficult conditions and hostility from without. The conditions had not changed, but the focus had. It is easy to become disheartened by the amount of rubbish that remains in us. The enemies of Nehemiah's project who looked on, hurling insults, recognized the obstacles of time and strength the workers faced and tried to use it discourage them: "What are these feeble Jews doing? Will they fortify themselves? Will they offer sacrifices? Will they complete it in a day? Will they revive the stones from the heaps of rubbish—stones that are burned?"[7] Temples are simply not built in a day!

My own experience has taught me that the main reason I didn't see my transformations is because I didn't know where to look for the elements involved in transformation. Gardeners know, because they tend and grow plants. Potters know, because they've handled clay. Our elders know because they've raised kids, survived catastrophes, and lived to tell about it. They are witnesses to the truth of Ralph Waldo Emerson's statement, "The years teach us much the days never knew."

There will be plenty of times in our spiritual journeys when we will lose hope and conclude that we are not changing, that God is not at work in our lives. At that time, the question to consider is whether we are going to believe 2 Corinthians 3.18, the scripture with which we began. Take a look at the verse again: "But we all, with unveiled face, beholding as in a mirror the glory of the Lord, are being transformed into the same image from glory to glory, just as by the Spirit of the Lord."

Think about each phrase for a moment before going on to the next, challenging your preconceived ideas on these thoughts:

- "We all"
- "Are being transformed"
- "Into the image of the glory of the Lord"
- "By the Spirit of the Lord"

My perspective is that "we all" includes you. No matter how imperfectly you feel you are walking out your faith, you are at all times in the midst of transformation. "Are being transformed" means that it is happening now, and it is happening *to* you. "Into the image of the glory of the Lord" reveals the finished product of our transformation: we are going to look like Christ! Finally, the most encouraging part: "By the Spirit of the Lord," transformation is being accomplished.

The Lifting of Veils

Two other phrases in this passage—"with unveiled faces" and "beholding as in a mirror"—invite us to dig a little deeper. The reference to an "unveiled face" is discussed a few verses earlier. It goes back to an event in Exodus where Moses' face shone brightly after meeting with God. He wore a veil because the Israelites could not bear to look upon the glory of God.[8] Verse 14 explains that the problem was not just the brightness to their eyes, but to their minds. They could not endure the intensity of God's presence, even in this reflected expression. In verses 15 and 16, Paul explains that in the same way, a veil covers our minds today, which keeps us from understanding the truth. He says this veil can be removed only by turning to the Lord.

A veil hides, separates and obstructs a clear view. When Paul says a veil is lifted when we turn to the Lord, he is not referring to a one-time thing. Throughout our spiritual journey, we turn again and again to the Lord. Even in Christ, we don't get the whole picture all at once. With each veil that lifts, we see less and less of ourselves and more and more of Him.

When he says, "We all with unveiled face are being transformed," I see two meanings: The first is that those of us whose faces are unveiled by turning to Christ are in a transformation process. The second is that *by the unveiling,* our transformations are realized. Sometimes light arrives to illuminate our faces like early morning seeping through the blinds without fanfare; other times, it is like an annoying early-riser, loudly lifting the blinds, forcing upon us a realization that is initially glaring and painful. This unveiling is the job of the Spirit and He has been known to work both ways.

The Torn Veil

There is further symbolism of the veil in the physical tabernacle and temple, an elaborate veil which separated the Holy Place from the Most Holy Place:

You shall make a veil woven of blue, purple, and scarlet thread, and fine woven linen. It shall be woven with an artistic design of cherubim. You shall hang it upon the four pillars of acacia wood overlaid with gold. Their hooks shall be gold, upon four sockets of silver. And you shall hang the veil from the clasps. Then you shall bring the ark of the Testimony in there, behind the veil. The veil shall be a divider for you between the Holy Place and the Most Holy.[9]

The veil in the Jewish temple created a physical barrier between God and man. It separated the people from the presence of God. Only one man, the High Priest, could enter into the Most Holy Place where God dwelt, and he could only do so once a year. At the moment of Jesus' death, that veil in the temple in Jerusalem ripped right down the middle, from top to bottom.[10] This miraculous and incredible event signified the removal of the barrier separating man from God. Hebrews 10.19–21 tells us that we may now have "boldness to enter the Holiest by the blood of Jesus, by a new and living way which He consecrated for us, through the veil, that is, *His flesh*." While He is lifting veils that obscure, and sometimes bestowing dramatic moments when He rips them from us, He now has become our veil that connects and reveals. He has become our vision, the matrix through which we view life.

I am reminded of the pivotal scene in C.S. Lewis' book *Til We Have Faces*, a retelling of the Greek myth of Cupid and Psyche, written from the perspective of a good and wise woman who has worn a veil for most of her life to cover her physical ugliness. She has spent her entire life writing a book that contains her charges against the gods, whom she blames for the loss of her beloved sister. One day she finds herself in a position to make her charge known to the gods but she finds she is holding a different, much smaller book than her own. When she begins to read it, it's not her carefully-written, logically-applied defense of herself against the gods' capriciousness toward humans coming from her mouth. Instead, she hears herself uttering the bitterness, jealousy and possessiveness in her heart, exposing the true spirit which had caused her sister to be lost. With shame, she realizes that this is finally her real voice, and that "we cannot come face to face with the gods 'til we *have* faces." When she finishes reading her guilt aloud, the judge says, "Are you answered?" And she knows that she is, for she says, "The complaint was the answer."[11]

In her complaint she found herself unveiled, both physically and spiritually, to reveal who she really was. In the terrible realization of truth, she expected condemnation, but the unveiling of her true face, while exposing blackness, also brought redemption. It is true for us as well: our complaints show others who we are while our unveilings show *us* who we are.

As in a Mirror

Author Gregory Maguire of *Wicked* fame writes in his book *Mirror Mirror*, "The thing about a mirror is this: The one who stares into it is condemned to consider the world from her own perspective."[12] This is the reality for physical mirrors. In contrast, the spiritual journey is all about seeing from God's perspective. The goal of transformation is not simply that you see from His perspective and not your own—though that is the blessing that occurs when we seek the face of God rather than consulting our own physical and mental reflections. The aim is that the more you see with spiritual eyes, the more you will see the glory of the Lord reflected in countless ways and places, as though in a mirror, and that your appearance will begin to look like that mirror-image of Christ, not yourself. The ultimate objective of a changed appearance is that the *world* might see Christ.

In the book *Practicing His Presence*, missionary Frank Laubach journals about his effort to spend every moment living in conscious awareness of, and in communication with, God. After two months, he wrote:

> Last Monday was the most completely successful day of my life to date ... and I remember how as I looked at people with a love God gave, they looked back and acted as though they wanted to go with me. I felt then that for a day I saw a little of that marvelous pull that Jesus had as He walked along the road day after day,

"God-intoxicated" and radiant with the endless communion of His soul with God.[13]

Laubauch's account of God-intoxication, which was tangible to others in just a few weeks, reveals this reflection aspect of Jesus. Others will see it but no one will be as amazed as you! It has an unwitting power and a joy no amount of self-improvement will produce.

There is a circular nature to transformation. As it unfolds before our eyes, we begin to understand how it has happened, which results in further transformation. Can you, for now, choose to believe Him when He says, "you *are* being transformed"? Even if you find that difficult, stick with me while we look at the deeper meanings found in God's dwelling places. I think you'll begin to recognize some evidence of your transformation into a Holy Temple.

3

Sanctuary

The Blueprints of Transformation

"And let them make me a sanctuary, that I may dwell among them."
Exodus 25.8

The first time I saw Cinderella's castle at Disney World, I was amazed at its size and intricate detail. I couldn't wait to get up close and see inside it, perhaps climb a spiral staircase to the top and view the park from one of the majestic towers. The exterior of the castle was magnificent, but I have to admit that I expected more. It appeared to me that this lavish pinnacle of the park was simply a façade towering over a beautiful but short tunnel. Since then, I have had the opportunity to visit real castles of substance, including *Neuschwanstein* in Bavaria, Germany—the inspiration behind Cinderella's castle—and famous cathedrals such as *Notre Dame de Paris*. Although I had no idea at the time, these imprints were critical in my continuing unawareness of the relevance of Paul declaring that we are temples of God.[1]

Words and pictures produce ideas which differ for each of us according to our imagination or experiences. Extensive teaching about the Bible tabernacle and temple had trained me to view these edifices from a standpoint of achieving perfection and righteousness by properly following instructions. Although 2 Corinthians 6.16 says, "We are the temple of the living God," I never grasped the seemingly obvious idea that being a temple of God meant He lived within me, but simply that we must be holy, which I understood to mean sinless. Though I knew many details about the tabernacle, I was definitely missing a wealth of insight.

It turned out that I was missing the intricacies of Cinderella's castle, as well. I later discovered that within the castle, but off-limit to regular guests, the castle contains Bibbidi Bobbidi Boutique (a hair salon for little princes and princesses), Cinderella's Castle Suite (a guest suite offered only to certain prizewinners), and Cinderella's Royal Table (a fanciful restaurant). Although it requires extra effort, extra money and maybe a little bit of *pixie dust* to experience these elements of the castle, they are the hidden inner truths concealed within the ornate exterior and the mosaic-tiled archway underneath.

What I have learned is that I was similarly mistaken about the dwelling places of God. From a tourist's perspective, my impression of temples, cathedrals and castles was that they were ornate and beautiful but uninhabited and unused, which bears little resemblance to God's idea of a temple. My notion of temples was obscuring the profound relevance God had embedded—through thousands of years of history and interaction with His people—in this word picture. It can be useful to examine your particular perceptions about sanctuaries for the purpose of eliminating preconceptions—and I encourage you to do that—but it is most important to see that to God, temples are complex, full of surprises, and a picture of our relationship with Him.

The Tabernacle: A Sanctuary in the Wilderness

While the Israelites were being led out of slavery in Egypt and journeying to their new home, it was necessary for God to reintroduce Himself and His ways to His people. They had been in Egypt for 400 years and though they knew *of* God, they didn't really know Him. The journey itself was a crash course on God. At Mount Sinai, God gave commandments for living and worshipping, including instructions for an elaborate tent—the tabernacle—that would travel with them and be their meeting place with Him.

Andrew Cross, who has built a business promoting the study of the tabernacle, says:

> Their concept of God was crude and confused. Remember that at the foot of Mt. Sinai, the Israelites bowed down and worshiped a golden Egyptian cow. They were forced to drink its powdered remains, but even before the bitter aftertaste was gone, God gave the Israelites something else to melt their gold into. God took them where they were at and channeled their creative energy into the construction of a place of real worship; where they could worship in Spirit and in Truth.
>
> The plans for this tent were inscribed by the hand of God on stone tablets right alongside the Ten Rules. If the Ten Rules present us with the terrifying holiness of God, and with an absolute and unchangeable standard by which our actions are judged, then the tabernacle presents us with God's love and invites us into His presence despite ourselves.[2]

The tabernacle was the center of Hebrew worship, an invitation into God's presence. Through an in-depth study of the tabernacle called *A Woman's Heart: God's Dwelling Place*,[3] by Beth Moore, I began to develop a fascination with this concept of an invitation from God to draw nearer to Him. The tabernacle period occurred while the Israelites were making a desert journey, which evolved—because of their disobedience—into forty years of wandering in the wilderness. An invitation from God is especially appealing when one is wandering in the desert!

My desert wanderings at that time included yet another ministry termination, the loss of not only our spiritual family but our best friends, a teenager who began acting out, and a husband who began choosing destructive coping mechanisms. I was suffering from Chronic Fatigue Syndrome and depression, caring for my two toddlers, and struggling to make ends meet during Steve's job transitions. Our financial difficulties became one of the avenues through which we began to see God's provision for us through others, as we often received from an unexpected source the exact amount of an unexpected bill. It was a good time to discover that God had provided a Helper and a Comforter who lived in me.

Another meaning of sanctuary—that of refuge—became particularly meaningful to me.

I knew that the inner part of the tabernacle contained a tent with two rooms. The first room was the Holy Place, where the priests carried out duties symbolic of forgiveness and connection with God. The other room, separated from the first one by a veil, was called the Holy of Holies, or The Most Holy Place. Only the High Priest entered this room, and only once a year. It was there, on the Mercy Seat of the Ark of the Covenant, that God dwelt. To enter without authorization meant death.[4]

What I did *not* know was that various scriptures show that every part of the tabernacle and of the whole worship and sanctification experience represented Jesus. He was and is the High Priest,[5] the sacrificial Lamb,[6] the veil,[7] the oil and light[8] in the lamp stand, the Mercy Seat,[9] and the showbread.[10] Moore furthered showed that every single element, down to the building materials used in the tabernacle, is used in reference to Christ elsewhere in scripture. Even the placement of the furniture was symbolic of Christ!

Nor did I grasp the personal significance of Hebrews 9.6–9, which contrasts the earthly tabernacle to another tabernacle:

> The Holy Spirit indicating that the way into the Holiest of All was not yet made manifest while the first tabernacle was still standing. It was symbolic for the present time…but Christ came as High Priest of the good things to come, with the greater and more perfect tabernacle not made with hands, that is, not of this creation.

The tabernacle was representative of something good to come, something greater and more perfect—some kind of spiritual tabernacle.

This information lay dormant inside of me for the next few years, as my life became an unlikely mix of aloneness and togetherness with God. A mountain stood before me which I could see no way to scale, nor did I try. I was simply too physically sick and emotionally broken. The only course of action I could take was to fix my eyes on God. Unlike in my earlier life of control and effort, I had the sense of "being journeyed." One day, I looked up to find myself on the other side of that mountain. I don't know how I got there, but I know with certainty that I did not accomplish it myself. As God had begun to open the eyes of my heart, I was surprised to realize that my highest highs had occurred in—and perhaps because of—my wilderness wanderings. It was during this time that I discovered the power of worship as the most reliable pain reliever possible and a likely point of entry for specific guidance and insight from God.

"Building" a Relationship

Several years later, while experiencing a bit more stability, the temple theme once again came to my attention. Though I was slowly healing and developing deepening intimacy with Christ, I still struggled for an explanation of the difficulties we had faced, as well as for strength to handle the current ones. I was beginning to look for and expect personal significance whenever I read about the temple, tabernacle, sanctuary or house of God. The more I did this, the more the concept of *relationship* began to jump out at me. I discovered five ways God's relationship with His sanctuary can be applied to my relationship with Him. I have come to think of these truths as the blueprints of the temple of God that I am becoming. We'll spend much of the remainder of this chapter discussing these five points.

Who Builds?

It was not until I understood the lopsided division of labor between us and God in the building of our temples that I first began to see the correlation between the temple and relationship. I had always thought it was my job to make myself into the Christian I was meant to be, which made me the builder rather than the building, but it was clear that God took credit and responsibility for His sanctuary; the temple was His idea, His design, His opus. He established His sanctuary: "You will bring them and plant them in the mountain of Your inheritance, the place, O Lord, which you have made for Your dwelling, the sanctuary, O Lord, which Your hands have established." [11]

And yet I also saw that God instructed the Israelites and Solomon to build the sanctuaries: "And let them make a sanctuary for Me, that I may dwell among them"[12]—this was the tabernacle. And, "Consider now, for the Lord has chosen you to build a house for the sanctuary; be strong, and do it"[13]—this was the temple. In both cases, the *people* built a physical structure to be the dwelling place for God.[14] This paradox indicates a joint effort between us and God in the establishment of our temples, but the ultimate acclaim was God's. He does not dwell in temples made "with hands,"[15] that is to say, built by men.

A simple way to understand this is to compare it to a couple who says "we are building a house." Most people who say this will not hammer a single nail. They will pick out a design and work with a builder who also says, "I am building a house." He will hire the construction crews to actually build the house. The couple is "building" because it is their house. They will own it. They will live in it. They have the final say in everything about it. When it comes to our temples, we are building the house, but as the initiator, designer, overseer, constructor and resident of my temple building project, God is the Master Builder.

The Basis of Spiritual Relationship: Holiness
A second link between the temple and relationship is the premium God placed on holiness within those temples. Holiness is relational in a very literal sense because it means to be *set apart*, indicating that something is dedicated for a specific purpose. To appropriate something in this way is to define its relationship with other things—to say, "It was previously used for that purpose, now it is devoted for this purpose." I had heard this from a young age, but somehow it translated to me as *perfect* or *righteous* in the area of obedience, something I must accomplish on my own because God cannot be in the presence of sin.

It is true that sin separates us from God, but it is because we have turned away from Him, not that He has turned away from us. His presence in me, as well as the very appearance of Jesus in a sin-filled world, attests to the relational and overcoming nature of holiness. Sin impedes intimacy, but He draws near despite that obstacle. Jesus bridges the gap, not simply in a general, impersonal plan to unite man to God if man can manage his own sin, but by penetrating each believer at the sin's source.

The difficulty I had in understanding holiness centered on the direction I faced in my set-apartness. I was more oriented toward what I was set apart *from* (sin, self, the world) than what I was set apart *to* (Jesus, our relationship, my purpose in this world). What personal holiness now means to me is growing in devotion to Him and to the purpose for which we are set apart (relationship with Him) so that I am able to be in relationship with a sinful world without "catching" their sin, just as Jesus could dwell with mankind and remain sinless. I find that the more committed I am to my relationship with Him and not just to His rules, the more the rules take care of themselves.

When I am *wholly* His, then I am *holy*. Wholeheartedly pursuing our purpose is far more effective at eliminating sin from our lives than simply relying on self-control. Frank Laubauch, the missionary who publicized the idea of living in total connection to God at every moment says of this endeavor, "This concentration upon God is strenuous, but everything else has ceased to be so."[16]

Besides having specific and detailed instructions for making it holy,[17] I noticed that God was in constant protection of His sanctuary against something He called "abominations": "'Therefore, as I live,' says the Lord GOD, 'surely, because you have defiled My sanctuary with all your detestable things and with all your abominations, therefore I will also diminish you; My eye will not spare, nor will I have any pity.'"[18] In the following verse, He warns of *pestilence, famine, exile* and *the sword* as consequences for a defiled sanctuary. This harsh language, which we will see again, is meant to convey the fiercely protective guardianship God had for His physical sanctuary, and also has now for us. If you fail to see that the heart of guardianship is *protection*, not *punishment*, you will miss the message about abominations, which will be discussed in greater detail in chapter 6.

Parenting is the closest thing we have to God's model of

guardianship. If I discover drugs in my child's room, I'm going to do whatever I can to remove the drugs, the source, the situations, and the emotional triggers that enabled his drug use. He will probably have to endure a period of exile, as well as a variety of other interventions. These actions will be perceived as punishment by him, but the ultimate goal is his physical, spiritual and emotional protection.

Ethereal Connections

A third connection of the early physical sanctuaries to relationship is that they represented a *true* tabernacle where Jesus dwells and ministers: "Now this is the main point of the things we are saying: We have such a High Priest, who is seated at the right hand of the throne of the Majesty in the heavens, a Minister of the sanctuary and of the true tabernacle which the Lord erected, and not man." [19]

The word "true" used here denotes a contrast to that which is fictitious or imagined, imperfect or frail. When people think of things that are *real* to them, they often think of those things they can see and touch, as opposed to the spiritual, which they cannot see. But the opposite is actually true: the physical tabernacle and temple, which could merely be seen, served as a "copy and a shadow of heavenly things." [20] Today there is a *true* sanctuary, which is multi-tiered, real and perfect (regardless of how it appears to us with our myopic vision):

- We have a sanctuary in the heavenly realm: "For He looked down from the height of His sanctuary; from heaven the Lord viewed the earth." [21] He is there now; it is where we will one day dwell with Him.

- His church is His sanctuary:

  Now, therefore, you are no longer strangers and foreigners, but fellow citizens with the saints and members of the household of God, having been built on the foundation of the apostles and prophets, Jesus Christ Himself being the chief cornerstone, in whom the whole building, being joined together, grows into a holy temple in the

Lord, in whom you also are being built together for a dwelling place of God in the Spirit.[22]

Did you notice the phrases "being joined together," "grows into," and "are being built"? These indicate action that is being done to us, even in the dynamic of a community of people.

• We are His sanctuary: "Do you not know that you are the temple of God and that the Spirit of God dwells in you?"[23]

Like three concentric circles, the spiritual tabernacle embodies the ultimate relationship, uniting us with Him and with each other in marvelous and unsearchable ways in this place and time, and simultaneously with our brothers and sisters from all places and times. As He dwells in us, each of our individual temples becomes a stone in the temple of His kingdom, allowing for increased communication of His purposes. His presence dwells in all levels of creation, in and among His people individually and together with each other and with the heavenly realm. The way God has flooded us with the concept of our lives as a temple illustrates that He intends for us to get the message—in case we missed it—of *Emanuel,* which means *God with us.* He wants us to see that not only is He *with* us, He is with *us.*

God has given us a tangible shadow of this spiritual reality. He has physically placed me within similar concentric circles of relationships: I am a citizen in the universe, the world, a nation, a city, a neighborhood, a church, a family and a marriage, as well as existing within a body. My body and those citizenships move in and out of these circles, performing multiple functions and impacting varying levels of the realms in which I exist. At times, I function in my community as part of a couple; other times, I act alone. My family interacts with my larger, extended family, or with another family.

While I have limited authority in even the lowest levels of my existence, God has complete authority, control and creativity in all realms equally, which He imparts to us as His purposes dictate. His presence and influence are vital at all levels, but particularly within the individual. He knows that His presence in the smallest unit will affect change all the way throughout the system. Like a foggy magnifying glass giving us a glimpse of what God is doing in the world, the physical temple hints at the mind-blowing connectedness of all things as they are being occupied and operated by God!

I hope I never stop discovering new aspects to the layers of the spiritual kingdom. When someone calls from out of the blue on the day of a terrible loss because they "had a feeling" something was wrong, I am aware of the living connections within the sanctuary of the kingdom. When two people or groups in prayer about a joint project come separately, but simultaneously, to the same solutions, I am reminded that they are not working alone. When someone prays for confirmation to a path God seems to be opening and a stranger on a plane unknowingly delivers the message of confirmation, I get very excited about the spiritual network of which I am a part.

The Power

A fourth correlation between relationship and sanctuary exists in the realm of power. Though Scripture and creation are full of the recognition of God's power, it was not until my study on the sanctuary that I began to connect that power with the growing relationship I had with Him. It seems like a no-brainer now: God established the sanctuary so that He might dwell among His people. The temple was only an empty structure until Solomon completed it and held a dedication service. While the people loudly praised and thanked God, "The house of the LORD was filled with a cloud … for the glory of the LORD filled the house of God." Solomon preached a sermon and prayed for God's presence in the temple and in the lives of His people. Then, "Fire came down from heaven and consumed the burnt offering and the sacrifices; and the glory of the LORD filled the temple."[24] The same thing happened when Moses completed the tabernacle.[25] If God is not there, all I have is an empty building. And if He is there, then something is going to be different in me.

King David recognized one manifestation of that power when

he struggled with the apparent victory of the ungodly, but he says, "When I thought how to understand this, it was too painful for me—until I went into the sanctuary of God; then I understood their end." [26] Why? Did simply entering into the temple give him miraculous knowledge or ease his pain? No, he poured out his heart to God in that place and God responded by sharing His perspective. David's physical circumstances generated mental anguish. I have that problem too! When I spend time in the place where God dwells within me, I get answers and I see the "big picture." In that place, focusing on the Who relieves me from the futility of why or how. Most of the time, it involves God drawing my attention away from others' guilt to my own. There is a song that says, "Turn your eyes upon Jesus. Look full in His wonderful face. And the things of earth will grow strangely dim, in the light of His glory and grace." [27] I don't know how He does this, but He does!

The Structure

By far the most wonderful and challenging aspect of "templehood" has been in my growing comprehension of the very structure of the sanctuary of God that I am, which is even more linked to relationship than any of the other points I have made. I mentioned earlier the Beth Moore study in which she showed that every element of the tabernacle is equated with Jesus Christ elsewhere in scripture. Remember, that tabernacle was a copy and a shadow of the true tabernacle. I began to ponder the idea that if I am a temple, I am somehow built *of* Christ.

Though I didn't grasp it fully at the time, I did find the concept that He is the temple hinted at in other places. In Psalm 20.2, David says:

> "May He send you help from the Sanctuary,
> And strengthen you out of Zion."

The couplet used here indicates two parallel statements. "Help" and "strength" are equal. Linguistically, "Sanctuary" and "Zion" must be equal or at least related.

Zion typically referred to Jerusalem or the mountain on which the city sat. In addition, the dwelling place of God is often named as Mt. Zion, which is equated with the entire spiritual realm, including Jesus Christ, in Hebrews 12.22–24. And when John says, "The Word became flesh and *dwelt* among us,"[29] he is using the Greek word *skenoo* for *dwelt*. *Skenoo* means "spread his tabernacle" among us. I cannot make a detailed case for this concept in this short treatise, but my experience has been that a willingness to consider this profound idea will invite the Spirit to develop it within you as you continue on your journey.

The Dilemma

Few of us are bold enough to believe that we are sufficiently Christlike to be a suitable dwelling place for God, nor do we find that His presence instantaneously and effortlessly makes us suitable. Despite His insistence that His people be holy as He is holy,[30] He takes up residence in decidedly unholy hearts and bodies, as all of us are when we first invite Him in. We've seen in Jesus' stablebirth that God specializes in humble beginnings, but the end He has planned is always spectacular. Not just any old place will do for the dwelling place of our God. If He's going to live there, He's going to be making some changes, and those changes are going to reveal Christ to us and in us. The question you are no doubt asking is *how?*

I realized one day while singing "O Lord, prepare me to be a sanctuary, pure and holy, tried and true. With thanksgiving, I'll be a living sanctuary for you,"[31] that I was actually asking Jesus to prepare my heart to be His dwelling place. I was asking Him to try it (test it) and make it true, and even agreeing to be thankful for the process. Of course, I didn't know what I was getting myself into, but it doesn't matter because even before I asked, He was already in there getting started. This song caused me to wonder if my struggles might somehow be correlated to this "preparing," no matter how unrelated or unjust they appeared to be. Eventually, I saw that the pain I had endured was a byproduct of the internal changes that had indeed prepared me to be a sanctuary in which the living God could reign with power. We'll see more about how that works in the following chapters.

I don't know if you've noticed that sometimes we have a tendency to want things our own way. We ask the Lord to purify us, prepare us, and change us, but we expect that to happen a certain way—in the manner of Merlin: "Abracadabra... poof... you're transformed!" or "At least," as my friend Chris says, "through a logical, clear, anesthetized process like... outpatient surgery!" This notion speaks to the universal effort to avoid pain, but sleeping through our growth process makes about as much sense as being put to sleep in order to endure an algebra class. Those who actually learned their algebra also learned that there was much more going on in that effort that would impact countless future habits and opportunities than the mere completion of math credits in order to graduate.

On the occasion of Jesus' transfiguration, it was not until Peter, James and John were "fully awake" that they saw His glory. [32] The prevalence of Jesus' use of the words "see" and "understand" are in direct opposition to the idea of fast-forwarding through our spiritual lives to the end. Transformation is not the time for sleeping. As Paul says in Romans 13.11, "It is *high time to awake out of sleep, for now our salvation is nearer than when we first believed.*"

4

Clean Sweep
Keep, Toss or Sell?

*"If we confess our sins, He is faithful and just to forgive us our sins
and to cleanse us from all unrighteousness."*

1 John 1.9

There is an easy-to-miss line in *The Lion King*[1] that amuses me
greatly. The Pridelands have fallen under the evil Scar's rule and
become desolate. The characters Pumbaa and Timon return with
Simba to his homeland. As they view the devastation from the
highest point in the land, Pumbaa mutters dryly to Timon, under
his breath so Simba can't hear, "Talk about your fixer-upper." I
always think of Jesus' perspective of the human heart when I hear
that assessment. We are definitely fixer-uppers.

In chapter one, I referred to the plethora of television shows
involving makeovers. There is one in particular, *Clean Sweep*,[2] in
which I found several spiritual parallels to my growing understanding of myself as a temple of God. In this show, homeowners have a room which is practically unusable. Overflowing with
stuff, the room is causing dysfunction in their lives and often their
marriage. Two teams come to save the day. One team assists the
family in emptying the room onto their lawn. Once the room is
empty, the second team begins to redecorate with specific focus
on the way this family lives (or wants to live).

As the room is vacated, the items are evaluated and placed in one of three piles, labeled "Keep," "Toss," and "Sell." The homeowners divide their belongings among the three areas with good-natured ribbing and encouragement from Team One. Always, always, always, when they are done, the "Keep" pile is too big. This time, the team gets serious. Going back through each item, they compel the homeowners to dig deeply to identify the function and value of each one, gently encouraging them to "let it go."

Eventually the "Toss" pile is hauled off and a yard sale eliminates the "Sell" pile. Occasionally the camera gives us a peek at Team Two's progress. On the last night of this three-day process, the couple goes to a hotel (usually with a box or two to sort), while the teams restock the newly decorated room with the couple's belongings. They return in the morning, exhausted, but anxiously awaiting the unveiling of their new domicile. They are delighted and amazed at the "transformation," and the teams scamper off for their next assignment.

Here is what I consistently noticed when I watched this show:

- People have a lot of junk! (This comforts me because although I also have a lot, these people have a lot more.)

- The homeowners are not having fun. Not only is it a monumental job to empty a room, but their junk is being revealed to their neighbors and the world. The emotional effort of making decisions is exhausting and, although they never show it, there is no way this is easy on the marriage! (How many couples have you known that agreed about what should be thrown away?)

- The team does not remove stuff from the "Keep" pile and "Toss" it without the homeowners' consent.

- The team never plays tug-of-war over an item, jerking it from the owner's hands and forcing them to let it go.

- The team does not get angry with the homeowners' stubborn grasp on worthless items, but they do gently and re-

lentlessly show them how such items are negatively affect-
ing their lives.

- It is a lot of work to do a clean sweep! But the homeowners
  are only doing the cleaning out—the remodeling/redeco-
  rating is being completely done by someone else.

- The result of a functional living space is worth the effort.

At first glance, this analogy seems to describe what God is in
the process of doing to make my heart suitable for His dwelling
place. He's doing a clean sweep, getting rid of the junk in my
heart, as was promised in 1 John 1.9: "If we confess our sins, He
is faithful and just to forgive us our sins and to cleanse us from all
unrighteousness."

Besides confession, we have some work to do as well. We have
a responsibility to remove what we are able to remove from our
cluttered temples. Jennifer Kennedy Dean says,

> Just as in the days of Hezekiah, when the priests removed every
> unclean thing from the temple to make it fit for the Lord (2
> Chronicles 29.16), so the Spirit of God is removing all unrigh-
> teousness and all flesh to make room for the presence of the Lord
> in your heart. He must be your heart's only inhabitant. "I will not
> yield my glory to another" (Isaiah 48.11). *What God instructed the
> priests through Hezekiah is your instruction: "Carry the uncleanness
> out from the holy place"* (2 Chronicles 29.5). He will not share His
> dwelling place. He will inhabit it alone. You were created to be
> His home, the place where His glory dwells. In the Old Testa-
> ment, the temple is a multilayered shadow of spiritual truth. It is
> a picture of Jesus, foretelling His death, burial and resurrection
> life. It is also the picture of each believer.[3]

We even see another clean sweep in Matthew 21. Near the
end of His ministry and life, Jesus is welcomed into the city of
Jerusalem and hailed as King. This is often called the "triumphant
entry." Normally, one might expect to hear an acceptance speech
at a time like that. Or perhaps, in His case, an explanation of their
error… after all, they were naming Him as their *physical* king,
and that was not His plan. Instead, His very first action was to

go to the temple, straight to the metaphorical heart of the matter, and clear out the merchants and what they were selling that was cluttering up His Father's house like so much junk.

The heart of Christ has always been tuned to the downtrodden, the poor and those in need of healing. The triumphant entry of Jesus occurred in the middle of the Feast of Passover, and many had come from far away for this annual celebration. They could not always bring their sacrificial animals with them, so some of the Jews had made a business of providing animals, changing various currencies and possibly providing food—all for a hefty profit. Seeing the worshippers taken advantage of in this way infuriated the Healer. He began turning over tables, casting out the moneychangers and driving out the animals and charlatans with a whip of cords. He said, "It is written, 'My house shall be called a house of prayer,' but you have made it a den of thieves."

This story is often called the "cleansing of the temple." His purging focused on those who were greedily profiting at the expense of the worshippers. Immediately after, He turned His attention to healing those who came to Him for help, the primary task He has set before Himself, this God who once referred to Himself as *Rapha*, the God Who Heals.

Though these stories appear consecutively in Scripture, I have never heard anyone make a connection between the triumphant entry of Jesus into Jerusalem, His cleansing of the temple, and His subsequent healing in the temple. Some might dismiss these links because the stories involved three different groups of people. Perhaps it only appears that they were consecutive events because nothing else was recorded between them, but I could not help seeing significance in a spiritual sense for us today because I saw myself in each group of people. And not just me. *We are each all three kinds of people at the same time:* people praising Him as our King, people full of all kinds of sinful and selfish motives, and people longing for healing.

Jesus stands at the door and knocks.[4] He doesn't force His way in like a SWAT Team. When we open the door, things immediately start changing. Perhaps the simplest, yet most critical medical knowledge known is that healing is facilitated when contaminants are removed from a wound. Any doctor who sees a splinter of wood, a piece of gravel, or mud in a cut will say, "This needs to come out." Forgiveness and the removal of obvious obstructions to our spiritual well-being is the ultimate goal of Jesus in the initial phase of cleaning us out.

But Wait—There's More!

When we first become Christians, we happily accept the forgiveness of our past sins and focus on cleaning up our bad habits: those visible sins in our lives and the unclean things we know we must remove, such as addictions, drunkenness and lying. We don't always do this very well. We hope that our efforts are eventually transferred to the heart issues we know are feeding our external actions, so we try hard to love rather than gossip, to not want to get drunk, to control not just our tongues, but our thoughts. We don't always do this well either. Over time, we will discover the malleable clay we were meant to be in the Potter's hands has been hardened to stone[5] deep within us and that even as we begin to experience periods of victory, the source of our struggle is at a core we cannot reach.

Discovery from the outside in is the natural order of things for us and is by God's design, I believe, because surrender is rarely our first instinct. Our hard heads require the opportunity to try and fail before we admit what is beyond our capabilities—and what is beyond my capability is changing the essence of *me*. The essence of me—and not just my behavior—is the flesh I am told not just to clean up, but to put to death, in symbolic parallel to His crucifixion.[6] Then, God says, "I will give you a new heart and put a new spirit within you; I will take the heart of stone out of your flesh and give you a heart of flesh."[7]

In my little fixer-upper in San Antonio, even $6,000 worth of renovations did not constitute a transformation. It was more inhabitable, but it had not changed from one form to another. Like others before me, I have discovered that a thorough cleaning out is not the total reality of transformation, it's just Phase 1. Writer

Anne Lamott tells this story:

> I heard Marianne Williamson say once that when you ask God into your life, you think he is going to come into your psychic house, look around, and see that you just need a new floor or better furniture and that everything needs just a little cleaning—and so you go along for the first six months thinking how nice life is now that God is there. Then you look out the window one day and see that there's a wrecking ball outside. It turns out that God actually thinks your whole foundation is shot and you're going to have to start over from scratch.[8]

Starting From Scratch

My mother is an excellent seamstress and she always said that she would rather completely start over on a project than have to repair a botched one or even continue with one that someone else started. When I set out to create something—a scrapbook, a favorite dish, or a painting—it's always easiest to start with a clean slate, new supplies, and an organized and well-stocked work area. Unfortunately, by the time we come to Jesus, we're damaged goods. We do not present Him with a clean slate.

Though He cleanses us from all unrighteousness, we learn very painfully that our initial cleansing does not miraculously transform us into the image of Christ. Many of us are surprised to find that we still struggle with the same temptations, and we fail to do and be all that we thought salvation would accomplish. So how do you begin from scratch on a building that has been condemned by the health department? The quickest way is just to bulldoze the whole thing (or go at it with Marianne Williamson's wrecking ball), but Jesus takes a kindlier approach. He dismantles it a little at a time in a process I call deconstruction.

It's important that you see that when He speaks of carrying the uncleanness out of the Holy Place, He is not just cleaning you out. *You* are the uncleanness; He is not even content to share this sanctuary with *you*. He is going to deconstruct you. He is building a place for Himself that *is* Himself. He isn't just trying to get a cozy spot to reside, but to replace *me* with *Him*. Earlier we looked at Ezekiel 5.11 where God seemed to be threatening punishment as a result of abominations in His temple. He said, "I will diminish you." With Jesus as my vision, I now see this as a holy promise. The more I see the truth about me, the more I *want* myself diminished!

You may be dismayed by the words *diminish, brokenness, wrecking ball, deconstruction* and *crucifixion.* Your self-esteem may not be up to hearing that your uncleanness is so entrenched even the waters of baptism don't get to the inner catacombs of you. It hurts to come to the realization that although you have tried to live a righteous life, be a good parent, child, wife or husband, you really are a mess! (Take heart! There's a reason God includes the messy stories of some of his favorite people—Abraham, Isaac, Moses, David—in the Bible.) Admittedly, deconstruction, demolition and crucifixion are not the usual selling points for this journey we are on, but anyone who sells you anything else is just not selling the whole package.

Each individual life contains the blueprint of maturity and even heroism, and an integral part of this will include death and rebirth. This concept is universally reflected in the myths, literature, religions, rites of passage and ceremonies of all cultures—as well as in the metaphors for growth we mentioned earlier—and this is precisely because it is God's elemental truth. We will not grow if our skin and bones are not stretched; we are not heroic if we haven't overcome anything hard.

Professor Arnold J. Toynbee, in studying the rise and disintegration of civilizations (and thus of human behavior) recorded his observations of this theme in *A Study of History.* He says,

> Schism in the soul, schism in the body social, will not be resolved by any scheme of return to the good old days (archaism), or by programs guaranteed to render an ideal projected future (futurism), or even by the most realistic, hardheaded work to weld together again the deteriorating elements. Only birth can conquer death—the birth, not of the old thing again, but of something new. Within the soul, within the body social, there must be—if we are to experience long survival—a continuous "recurrence of birth" to nullify the unremitting recurrences of death. For it is

by means of our own victories, if we are not regenerated, that the work of Nemesis is wrought: doom breaks from the shell of our very virtue. Peace then is a snare; war is a snare; change is a snare; permanence is a snare. When our day is come for the victory of death, death closes in; there is nothing we can do, except be crucified—and resurrected; dismembered totally, and then reborn.[9]

The knowledge of this death is vital if we are to recognize it when it occurs, yet it is imperative that we do not focus more on the death than the rebirth. We will discover universal elements in each other's experiences but we cannot know the exact forms this death will take in our own lives, and preoccupation with those possibilities can only result in more resistance and rigidity.

We will be discussing the breathtaking rewards and appearance of rebirth in further chapters, but for now I will leave you with the exciting promise of Ephesians 1.18–20: the promise that when our eyes are opened, there we will find, among other treasures, "enlightenment ... hope ... and the riches of the glory of His inheritance in the saints, the exceeding greatness of His power toward us who believe, according to the working of His mighty power which He worked in Christ when He raised Him from the dead and seated Him at His right hand in the heavenly places."

Did you catch that? The very same power that raised Jesus from the dead—available to you and me! And the best part is seeing in your flesh the source of all this power—Christ—and realizing that it has been there all along.

Even though spiritually I'm bound for more than a little dusting and polishing, the lessons I learned from the television show *Clean Sweep* are still applicable. Deconstruction is handled in the same way, with each junky belonging under consideration completely up to me to surrender. The hard part is that each of those items is a chunk of me, and that's why it hurts so badly.

In their song "Surrender," the group BarlowGirl sings about God asking a woman to surrender her dreams. And even though she knows she should and that He will do something beautiful with them, she explains why it's so difficult:

"Surrender, surrender," you whisper gently
You say I will be free
I know, but can't you see?
My dreams are me. [10]

There are certain things that just seem to go together: rainy days and hot chocolate, camping and bug bites, me and my...*self.* I cling to myself the way a wary traveler who was once robbed and left stranded in a foreign country guards his wallet—possessively, protectively, and even suspiciously.

I am that wary traveler in more ways than one. Although I was not in a foreign country when I was robbed—I was vacationing in Galveston, Texas—my oldest daughter and I were skeptical for months of anyone who wanted to admire my baby daughter, since that is how the thief who stole my purse distracted us. We began to guard not only our belongings, but the gateway through which those belongings had been stolen so that thereafter, not even baby-admirers were above suspicion. Because life, from the moment we're born, often seems to be one attack after another at our hearts, we become, in a word, *untrusting.*

We are desperately attached to ourselves and to all that is us because all of us have felt invisible, passed-over, neglected, or rejected. We're struggling so much for our existence and our identity that we want to hold on to each part for dear life—ours—even when we get the sneaking suspicion that Something Bigger seems determined to make us part ways!

In the next chapter, we're going to see what deconstruction looks like. As we do, try to remember the goal of a clean sweep: those dysfunctional rooms—and you—are being transformed into something better than they are!

5

Falling Apart
Between Invitation and Healing

Whatever happened to the young man's heart
Swallowed by pain, as he slowly fell apart?

Shinedown

When my oldest daughter was little, I taught her how to make words with ABC blocks. At four, she was spelling out her name and brilliant phrases like "I Love Mommy," alternating the colors the way I showed her to maximize the effect. So cute. (I'm kidding about the colors!) Ten years later, my two younger children could not be bothered with those odd symbols on the alphabet blocks, which clearly had nothing to do with the real purpose of the blocks: to build a tower as tall as they could, then find creative ways to knock it over. They always won because even if the tower fell before it was finished, their objective of destruction was still met. Building it was not the point at all. Nowadays they all play a slightly more grown-up game of blocks called Jenga, wherein they pretend they don't want the wooden sticks to fall, but everyone is secretly anticipating the climactic crash!

Ah, for the good old days when demolition was fun; that is to say, when it was something you did, not something you endured.

I want you to consider for a moment two different scenarios involving the same variable: a list of symptoms. If you researched a disease and read the list of symptoms, it would be alarming, but if you *had* the symptoms and didn't know why, discovering the list would actually be a relief. Even if the disease was serious, you would at least have an answer and be in a position to become proactive. This is how I felt when I read a book on the so-called *terrible twos*. I was relieved to know that what my daughter was doing was not only normal, but developmentally necessary. This is also how I felt about my spiritual journey. I had experienced symptoms of anxiety, fear, conflict, depression, illness, anger, and so much more, but I had no idea to what condition they were related.

The Temple

We've considered the Old Testament tabernacle. Now we're going to take a brief look at the New Testament temple. To fully understand deconstruction, you need to know that the temple was a magnificent permanent structure which replaced the portable tabernacle. It was built by King Solomon in Jerusalem in 960 BC over a period of seven years. Like the tabernacle, it contained an inner sanctuary called The Most Holy Place that was separated from the Holy Place by a veil. In contrast to the tabernacle era, the temple era represented a kind of settled-ness on God's part—it had "survived" for a thousand years by Jesus' day—despite the fact that it had fallen into disrepair more than once during the Jews' tumultuous history. It was destroyed by the Babylonians in 586 BC and rebuilt under the leadership of Ezra in 515 BC At that time, Daniel called the broken-down temple "desolate" and prayed that the Lord's face would shine on His sanctuary.[1]

By the time of Christ, the temple was the pride of the Jews, and was pivotal in their worship, yet many changes had occurred in the years since they had folded up the tabernacle for the last time. The Jewish religion and lifestyle had deteriorated. They were living under Roman occupation. They had begun to put more credence in interpretations and traditions than in God's word. There was corruption in the priesthood, stark divisions among the people, and the temple had become a veritable marketplace.

Shortly after seeing a correlation in Matthew 21 between the events relating to the temple and God's people (declaration of Jesus as king, cleansing of the temple, healing), I came to Matthew 23 where Jesus, who had begun preaching in the temple, lamented Jerusalem's spiritual state. In verse 38 He says, "See! Your house is left to you desolate!" My interest was piqued because of my familiarity with Daniel's use of the word "desolate" to describe the temple as it lay in ruins. And yet, at this time, the temple had been rebuilt for many years and was a busy center of Jewish culture. The disciples had heard this statement so perhaps that is why, as they left the temple with Jesus, they "showed Him the buildings of the temple."[2] I suspect it was really more of a question: "What do you mean 'desolate?' The temple looks fine!"

In reply to their question, Jesus foretells the emotional, spiritual, physical and political events surrounding the destruction of the temple and of Jerusalem. For the Jews, this event would be catastrophic, a massive blow to their religious system, which had been in place for thousands of years. It would have felt like the end of their world, and in many ways, it was. We know the rest of the story, the introduction of a Savior, so we are aware that the destruction of the Jewish temple was representative of the necessary removal of an old, imperfect system that had fulfilled its purpose and was being removed for the inauguration of a better covenant.[3]

Even before I saw how this picture related to me, I had a strong sense of déjà vu as I read about the impact this tragedy would have on God's people. He didn't tell the how, when or why; He told them how it would *feel*. It appears that calamities of every kind, big and small, produce similar responses because the destruction of the temple would seemingly be accompanied by the same kind of emotional fall-out I experienced when my best friend moved away or when my children make scary choices. I realized, with awe, that if I am a temple of God, and if I had experienced the emotions, trauma and rewards Jesus said would be associated with temple destruction, then it seemed likely that the events which had caused my suffering were part of a planned, developmental stage in my temple building; namely, deconstruction.

Austrian Holocaust survivor Victor Frankl believed that once suffering achieves meaning, it ceases to be suffering. This was that moment for me, when all the randomness of my suffering came together in one meaningful package. I saw how God was connected with my suffering in a positive way, how these events had changed me for the better and how they had deepened my relationship with Him. I saw Matthew 24 as code for how it feels to be transformed. The events of the process described there have happened to me many times, teaching me that transformation occurs in many phases.

Deconstruction
We're going to take Mathew 24 apart, bit by bit. You may not undergo each of the elements we will be discussing every time Jesus begins a new phase of transformation in you, but I do guarantee that every one of them is an indicator of transformative work. I recommend that you read along in your Bible as we work our way through the text. It will help you get a clearer picture of this portrait of significant change. Remember to think of yourself as a temple-in-progress as we look at thirteen symptoms of spiritual deconstruction.

Destruction – "I tell you the truth, not one stone here will be left on another; every one will be thrown down" (v 2).

Jesus gets straight to the bottom line when asked about the temple buildings: a destruction will occur, a complete demolition, down to the foundation; every stone will be removed.[4] If the physical temple had to be removed for something better, it makes sense that my unworthy sanctuary also needs to come down to make way for something better in me. This type of deconstruction is a purposeful and systematic dismantling and removal of things that do not belong in a holy temple, followed by rebuilding. Looking back, I had no way of knowing that the finished product was going to be a phenomenal improvement on my current hovel, so the day I first looked out my front door and saw the wrecking ball in the yard was very unnerving.

Deception – "And Jesus answered and said to them: 'Take heed that no one deceives you'" (v 4).

Because I had been learning about spiritual warfare and Satan's devices, I could not think of deception without immediately knowing the source of that. Satan's ability to confuse us is as pervasive as the kudzu vine which can cloak an entire forest like a blanket, obscuring, fusing and strangling. Like kudzu, he is only able to do this where the environment is favorable. He is enormously interested in how I respond to deconstruction; he does not want me to see what is happening on a spiritual level. Just as Satan tried to get Eve to question God's desire for her life, he does a pretty good job of hiding God's desire for me, too.

Satan's initial deception lies in the misdirection of our attention toward external circumstances and our failure to recognize those circumstances as the very platform on which our transformations will occur. In other words, we think what we're experiencing is merely the loss of a job, the rebellion of our teenager, or the diagnosis of cancer. These are very real and frightening events, but in every one of them God wants to move us toward a different place.

Every circumstance in which we find ourselves is a stage on which to "try" our sanctuaries, a setting for this new chapter in our story. Whenever I find myself thinking, "I could be a good Christian if it weren't for these circumstances I'm in," Satan's been at work. The majority of my transformation has occurred in the arenas of personal failure, marriage, parenting, illness, difficult church dynamics, and so on. Over the years these arenas have exposed in me a rebellious heart, selfishness, pride, fear, a lack of trust in God, and many other unattractive things. Transformation requires that you look no further than at what is already present in your life, and that is why Satan misdirects our attention.

Our second deception often includes thoughts about why this is happening to us. This is frequently where we begin to blame God, others or ourselves. As previously discussed, Romans 12.2 tells us that transformation is realized by the renewing of our minds. One of the ways we participate in this monumental task is by constantly seeking to annihilate any falsehoods lurking in the nooks and crannies of our thinking. Difficulties bring these false beliefs to the surface where we can become aware of them. While we may rightly conclude that God is at work in the midst of a struggle, this is far different from blaming Him. Blaming ourselves and others not only distracts from God's purposes, it creates pain, conflict and serious hindrances to our spiritual vision.

Third, we tend to underestimate what we can tolerate. Satan says, "You can't handle this... this is too much to bear... it's hopeless." History shows the extraordinary resilience of humans to endure far beyond what they imagine possible. Because of the strength of Christ,[5] we are all stronger than we think we are! I used to be emotionally fragile and overly sensitive much of the time, and struggled every day with the perceived difficulty of my life. In recent years I have learned to focus on my imputed strength, and most days, that is my default. I have learned that when I say, "I just can't take this," I can't! My periods of doing what psychologist and author David Schnarch calls "awfulizing"[6] have become fewer and further in between.

When I look back at all I have survived, I now know no matter what hits next, I *can* take it, one way or another. The question is *how* will I survive it? I have two choices. I can give up (or barely hang on), believing I'm not strong, experiencing "secondary infections" of depression, illness and more, or I can challenge this lie of Satan, claim the strength I own because I am in Christ, and make sure all my thinking is based on the truth that "He who is in me is greater than he who is in the world."[7]

Unfortunately, when difficulties come too quickly or too many at a time, my newly-gained ability to withstand the deception defaults to fleshly reactions and before too long, I realize I have let go of Jesus' hand and have depended on something other than Him for strength. My self-deception radar will always be dependent on a close walk with Christ, for it is Christ who is greater than "he who is in the world," not me! There is truth in Oswald Chambers' statement: "Watch how God will wither up your confidence in natural virtues after sanctification, and in any power you have, until you learn to draw your life from the reservoir of the resurrection life of Jesus."[8]

It is possible to be deceived about this process even when we understand how it works, as I have discovered numerous times. A warning is necessary if you, like me, lean toward implementing this simply as a rational formula rather than recognizing the mystery of the numinous power at work in our souls and in our world. If Satan can get us to default to the process rather than clinging to Jesus when our foundations start shaking, we will soon find that we have tried to make it on our own again.

Anxiety – "You will hear of wars and rumors of wars" (v 6).

In political terms, we call wars and rumors of wars *unrest;* emotionally, we call it anxiety. It is usually at this stage of secondary infection that I begin to hear a faint alarm in the distance, and to suspect both a new construction phase and the presence of deception. When Jesus starts prying stones out or chiseling away at stubborn mortar, we can't avoid discomfort. To completely change from one paradigm to another is extremely uncomfortable!

Anxiety is so common in us that we often give little significance to it until it requires medication, but this scripture indicates that anxiety is a signal that God is trying to get our attention. What if we didn't tune it out by eating, turning on the television, taking a nap, or having a drink?

Kierkegaard defined anxiety as "the inevitable, spiritual state of man standing in the paradoxical situation of freedom and finiteness."[9] That is a fancy way of saying that when we recognize our smallness in the universe, we are at the same time in a position to also recognize our freedom in infinity (through Christ). He says: "Learning to know anxiety is an adventure which every human must go through—to learn to be anxious in order that he may not perish, either by never having been in anxiety or by succumbing to anxiety. Whoever has learned to be in anxiety in the right way has learned the ultimate."[10] This unexpected link between anxiety and freedom challenges us to examine or confront our anxiety. The freedom at the end of each deconstruction period seems so distant and uncertain in its early stages that insecurity naturally results when the process is put in motion.

Fear – "See to it that you are not alarmed" (v 6).

Jesus knows unrest is troubling, alarming, and frightening. Some people feel anxiety and then they feel troubled about feeling anxiety, effectively doubling their apprehension. What is called for when we experience anxiety is confrontation; to be, as Kierkegaard said, "rightly *in* anxiety." *Confront* literally means *to stand face to face with*. It doesn't always have the aggressive connotation we sometimes infer, but rather the willingness to be present with something, not to run from it. Thus we are most cooperative with God's transformative methods when we do not seek to suppress our feelings of anxiety, but to watch and wait for the revelation of His purposes which they reflect.

I recently learned that the scriptures contain 365 instances of the command not to be afraid. That's one reminder for every day of the year! In my younger years, when I thought feelings were reflections of reality, I could never understand Jesus telling us to *not* feel what we feel. Then I noticed that every time He says "fear not," there is something legitimate to be afraid of. I think there must be so many reminders about fear in Scripture because deep down, we're all desperately afraid. But I have to believe that when God says "fear not," it indicates that He knows something we don't. Not only does He know the outcome and has declared that "all things [will] work together for good," He also knows the blinding, paralyzing impact fear has on us.

Understand – "See that you are not alarmed; for all these things must come to pass, but the end is not yet" (v 6).

Jesus wants us to replace our fear with the understanding that these things have to happen in order for an important change to take place. Knowing there's a purpose behind an event eases its difficulty somewhat. Say you were taking the SAT. Even though you don't enjoy taking the SAT and it creates stress in your life, it doesn't bring confusion into your life. You understand it as a necessary step in getting in to college. You don't ask, "Why is this happening to me?" But say you were charged unjustly with cheating on the SAT exam. False charges also create stress, but this time, the stress arises from the indignation and outrage you feel at the unfairness to which you feel you are being subjected. In our culture, especially, justice is considered a birthright, and when it is threatened, we are incredulous and confused about how it could happen, how it will impact our future, how we are to clear our name. We ask the questions, "Why is this happening to me?" and "What did I do to deserve this?"

In God's scheme of things, even false charges become useful in the process He is implementing in us. Perhaps we truly did nothing to deserve the circumstances in which we find ourselves. But rather than inhibit our ability to endure it by adding confusion, Jesus says that trials and tribulation, and the fear and anxiety they produce, should alert us to His redeeming work in the building of our temples. In a calamity or crisis, at whatever point we are, we can safely say, "The end is not yet." That knowledge has the power to quell those anxieties so we can more clearly see what God is trying to show us.

War, Famine, Pestilence and Earthquakes – "For nation will rise against nation, and kingdom against kingdom. And there will be famines, pestilences, and earthquakes in various places. All these are the beginning of sorrows" (vv 7–8).

When we bring it down to a personal level, we can all remember times we've experienced periods of warring emotions and relationships at war. (In my case, the times I *wasn't* experiencing them would be easier to list!). James 4.1 tells us that wars and fights among us are reflections of internal war within our own members, so an increase in conflict with others is not uncommon as change begins to occur. I asked you in chapter three to remember the words "famine," "pestilence" and "earthquake" from the passage in Ezekiel as consequences of God dealing out punishment for the defilement of and abominations in the sanctuary. In symbolic ways, these things are the consequences I will experience in my own spiritual sanctuary when there are abominations Jesus is trying to remove.

Every Christian experiences spiritual dry spells. These are the spiritual famines and pestilence (disease), which are common outgrowths of war. Usually we feel vaguely guilty when our spiritual life seems stagnant; I say *vaguely* because during dry spells we're often numb, so anything we feel will be vague. But dry spells are an inevitable and natural indicator of God at work in us.

In *Dark Night of the Soul,*[11] St. John of the Cross suggests that God uses spiritual aridity to develop a thirst for Him. In the context of psychology, dryness can also represent numbness, which is a clear sign that we have shut down something painful we want to avoid, such as our anxieties and fears. What we begin to learn is that the more we suppress and ignore the messages found in the tools of fear and anxiety, the more intense God often allows it to get in order to get our attention.

A Whole Lotta Shakin' Goin' On

Jesus also promises earthquakes. As a person who likes things to be calm, change has always been difficult for me. Until I understood the purpose of spiritual, emotional and relational earthquakes, I *hated* them. (Now I just intensely loathe them!) But I've come to see that churches, relationships and especially individuals *need* earthquakes. I think of it as God saying, "Do I have your attention now?"

In Exodus 15.17 we saw that God's sanctuary was a mountain. In Hebrews 12, a contrast is described between the events at Mount Sinai, when Moses was on the mountain receiving the law, and our coming to the Holy Mountain of God (Mount Zion). This contrast represents the difference between law (Mount Sinai) and Christ (Mount Zion), and the choice we must make between the two.

> For you have not come to the mountain that may be touched and that burned with fire, and to blackness and darkness and tempest, and the sound of a trumpet and the voice of words, so that those who heard it begged that the word should not be spoken to them anymore....
>
> But you have come to Mount Zion and ... to Jesus the Mediator of the new covenant. ...See that you do not refuse Him who speaks. For if they did not escape who refused Him who spoke

on earth, much more shall we not escape if we turn away from Him who speaks from heaven, whose voice then shook the earth; but now He has promised, saying, "Yet once more I shake not only the earth, but also heaven."

Now this, "Yet once more," indicates the removal of those things that are being shaken, as of things that are made, that the things which cannot be shaken may remain. Therefore, since we are receiving a kingdom which cannot be shaken, let us have grace, by which we may serve God acceptably with reverence and godly fear.[12]

Mount Sinai was engulfed in dark clouds, lightning, thunder and earthquakes while Moses met with God.[13] The Hebrew writer says we haven't come to *that* mountain, but we have come to Mount Zion. He says not to be like those who refused God's voice at Mount Sinai, but to hear the voice that will shake more than just the earth. Jesus promises more shakings for a very important reason: to remove anything that can be removed, so that "*what cannot be shaken* may remain." Earthquakes are inescapably linked with the kingdom we are receiving in ourselves because He wants to show us how much of our building (structure) is improperly built and hindering His building (process).

Paul describes this process in 1 Corinthians 3.9–16:

You are God's building. According to the grace of God which was given to me, as a wise master builder I have laid the foundation, and another builds on it. But let each one take heed how he builds on it. For no other foundation can anyone lay than that which is laid, which is Jesus Christ. Now if anyone builds on this foundation with gold, silver, precious stones, wood, hay, straw, each one's work will become clear, for the Day will declare it, because it will be revealed by fire; and the fire will test each one's work, of what sort it is. If anyone's work which he has built on it endures, he will receive a reward. If anyone's work is burned, he will suffer loss, but he himself will be saved, yet so as through fire. Do you not know that you are the temple of God and that the Spirit of God dwells in you?

Though he uses the metaphor of fire rather than earthquakes, it is quite clear that we build, but a day will come when some kind of trial will reveal the materials we have used. Though we may suffer loss, it is not to our eternal damnation, but simply to assure that the building is built properly. This is the experience of every Christian: thinking we've come a long way spiritually only to discover through a difficulty how little faith (or self-control, or patience, or love) we really have.

"He came to shake us and to wake us up to something more than what we've always settled for," says Nichole Nordeman in her song "Live."[14] If we understand that "shakings" are a natural part of receiving within us a kingdom that cannot be shaken, then we can receive those shakings, as Hebrews says, with grace (v 28). The Prince of Peace did not come to bring peace, but a sword, and His chief area of work is in the souls of men, "piercing between joint and marrow."[15] Recall also that the sword was included in Ezekiel 5.11 among the consequences of desecrating God's sanctuary.

Beginnings – "All these are the beginning of birth pains" (v 8).

Whenever things start to feel crazy in my life, I now see the emotional and spiritual upheaval for what it is: the *beginning* of a new construction zone in me. I'm just getting started! But note that Jesus is now comparing the deconstruction process to childbirth. We women have quite a relationship with our labor experience—it is the second thing everybody wants to know about after they hear the baby is doing well. Perhaps this is because the long-awaited and dreaded experience is so powerfully connected to life and spiritual matters.

When I went into labor with my daughter, the contractions were three minutes apart rather than the ten or so I had been promised, and transitioned quickly to one minute apart. This was rather alarming, especially since I had committed to a drug-free delivery at a birthing center. I wondered, "If things are this bad now, will I be able to get through the hard part without anesthesia?" I began to think what most women think at the first intense contraction: "I've changed my mind! I don't want to do this!" At that moment, I experienced a new personal best in anxiety and fear. What was interesting to me later was that though I knew full well what was going on as I went *into* labor, *during* labor I had no ability to connect the pain with the idea of a baby. I had to be reminded of the purpose of my suffering frequently ("Gina, you're having a baby!")—and it surprised me every time.

Through the events of our lives, we are each being drawn deeper into relationship with God. Like a birth, these events move us from one phase of our life to another, each one increasingly toward life and freedom, but the crossing is not without its discomforts. When anxiety and fear are present in our lives, we must remind *ourselves* and *each other* of the presence of an impending birth and the necessity of difficult passages to bring something to life. We must look to our focal point (Christ), do our breathing (Holy Spirit) and surround ourselves with a few good labor coaches so we can remember that *God is trying to bring something to life in this struggle.*

Persecution – "Then you will be handed over to be persecuted and put to death, and you will be hated by all nations because of me" (vv 9–11).

Next Jesus tells of the role outsiders sometimes play in this process. He lists offenses, persecution, hatred, betrayal, and even death. Satan tries to use whoever he can to derail the intended progress of this process, but God is also using them in the transformation process. The death at stake always includes the elimination of some part of us for replacement with Christ, but it might include the death of relationships or long-held dreams, or the loss of any number of tangible things in our lives. Note that these losses are not always going to be sinful things in your life.

There was about a decade when Steve and I felt very much under persecution. I am a little leery of calling it persecution now, but at the time, it was difficult to see it any other way. When earnest seeking is perceived as dishonesty and answered with lies, trumped-up charges, and jury-rigged committee meetings designed to tip the scales against us, it felt very undeserved, malicious and even life-threatening, in the broader sense. We were not faultless in these exchanges, but being unable to reconcile our crimes with our persecution led to a prolonged period of depression for us, and especially for Steve. Rejection and betrayal by close friends and the very ones we sought to serve cut deep. It took a long time to realize that nothing put me closer to the heart of Christ than betrayal. I have come to believe that this suffering of Christ's is one we absolutely must share.

David mourned, "Even my close friend, whom I trusted, he who shared my bread, has lifted his heel against me."[16] These elements of trust and fellowship are what cause the unique pain of betrayal. *Only* a friend can betray us. We might be able to convince ourselves that some offenses don't hurt, but betrayal strips away all pretenses of invincibility as it inflicts what Shakespeare called "the most unkindest cut of all,"[17] causing them to become watershed moments in our lives.

In his song "Anthem," Leonard Cohen brings hope into the heart of betrayal: "Everything is cracked, that's how the light gets in."[18] If we can find any beauty in something as painful as betrayal, it would be this: it gives Jesus an ideal entry point for His work. Yet, ironically, betrayals often close us up, sealing off His access. If we allow betrayal to be used by Jesus for deep healing, not just of the betrayal, but of past wounds that inevitably get tangled up with it, I am convinced we will avoid the bitterness that often sets in afterwards, keeping ourselves free to experience joy.

Sometimes we can perceive persecution, hatred and betrayal where none is intended, but whether perceived or real, they have a tremendous impact on us. It isn't a conclusion we draw easily, but feelings of being hated and mistreated are connected to God's work in us. As we realize what is being revealed in us as we are shaken up, and surrender to that work, it will always become apparent that whether the persecution, hatred and betrayal are actual or imagined, there was something for us to learn about ourselves.

Defining Moments – "And because lawlessness will abound, the love of many will grow cold, but he who endures to the end shall be saved" (vv 12–13).

This is that climax or "point of decision" that Donald Miller says is present in every story. In temple deconstruction, this is only one of many defining moments. It is easy to react sinfully to the wrong that others commit against us. In difficult job situations, roommate dynamics, friendships, churches, and especially marriages, the tension that always surrounds change or the need for change will be intolerable for some and they will bail, emotionally or physically. My own experience has been that when I attempt not to feel that apprehension, I shut myself off from *all* emotions, especially love. This is a form of quitting, even if I don't actually leave. To quit when times gets tough is to experience the work He is doing in us without any of the blessings at the end. This is as crazy as telling your dentist three-fourths of the way through a root canal that you want to leave.

In the situation Steve and I were in with our church, we focused on the hurtful actions of others and concluded that God also had abandoned us. So we all but abandoned Him at that point, effectively drawing out this period of darkness. We experienced Emerson Hart's earthbound take on kite-flying: "I don't remember when we ran out of rope, but when we did we lost all hope. We just stood there crying. That's what we learned about flying." [19] It was many years later before we saw how this painful treatment from our spiritual family actually led to the true spiritual flight that is found *only* when our rope runs out.

I recently received an email from my friend Ethan who was struggling with his faith. He gave me permission to share: "When Christ found me, it was a pretty amazing time. Not because everything suddenly became wonderful, but because there was that "spirit," that peace that held me even when everything was falling apart… which is why I gave my testimony. After the testimony last year, my life began being systematically dismantled. Since this email isn't really intended to be a whine fest, I'll spare you the details. Suffice it to say that all the support networks I had evaporated for one reason or another." He went on to list the very serious struggles he was facing with depression, suicidal tendencies and sexual temptation.

In the midst of my empathy for Ethan's pain, I recognized an important and familiar phrase and connection: "After my testimony last year," (public pronouncement of Jesus as His Lord), "my life began being *systematically dismantled*" (everything seemed to be falling apart). He was experiencing deconstruction but couldn't see the bigger picture while in the middle of the demolition! As Ethan struggled with unanswered prayers and very real pain, it was not uncommon to hear him say, "I'm done," or "It's over," or "I've had all I can take." But several days later, there he would be, still hanging on by that fragile faith, through which he was continually reminded that there was no other avenue that could truly deliver him, though he considered many. I had no doubt what was happening to Ethan, nor what would be the conclusion of the matter: in a word, transformation. Dismantling is the precursor to building, and we will always be faced with a decision when it gets painful: Do I stay or do I go?

The faces of choice are as varied as there are opportunities to decide. It might be the decision to obey, to trust, to stand firm, to hold on, to let go, to wait, to risk, to love, to forgive, to open up, or to be silent. Victory is found in thousands of small decisions like these made in the heart and mind, not necessarily in grand, public resolutions and gestures. Because it is such an enormous part of the deconstruction process, we will look more in-depth at the topic of defining moments in chapter 8.

Ministry – "And this gospel of the kingdom will be preached in all the world as a witness to all the nations" (v 14).

Jesus tells how this experience—this "good news"—will be preached as a witness to all people. How true that has been for Steve and me! Because the end result was so amazing, this particular period of deconstruction has been a part of our message ever since! Amazingly, only a week or so after I heard from Ethan, he was ministering Christ to me in my own low moment. I asked him about the miraculous turnaround. He said, "I'm just holding on to truth." It seems ministry is often nothing more than reminding others, through our stories, to hold on; it is, as Henri Nouwen said, "The profession of fools and clowns telling everyone who has ears to hear and eyes to see that life is not a problem to be solved, but a mystery to be entered into." [20]

Abominations and Desolations – "Therefore when you see the 'abomination of desolation,' spoken of by Daniel the prophet, standing in the holy place, then let those who are in Judea flee to the mountains" (v 15).

The next thing that happens is seeing the Abomination of Desolation. These were among the words to remember from Daniel 9 and Ezekiel 5. For the original audience, this was the desecration of their holy temple and its sacred elements by their enemies. That's what it is for us as well. We are made up of stones that do not belong in a Holy Temple, stones which need crucifying, which the process is leading us to see. It is at this point we begin to agree with psychologist Carl Jung's insight: "To become acquainted with oneself is a terrible shock." [21]

Part of the reluctance to face our Abominations of Desolation is shame. The unbearable shame of seeing our true spiritual condition is only possible to accept if we pair it with a solid understanding of the cleansing of Christ. Without that, we could not bear to know who we are, but without knowing who we are, we can't truly appreciate the miracle of grace. It is in the tension between the extremes of *simul justus et peccator* [22] ("righteous and at the same time a sinner") that we wrestle and come to terms with who we are in Christ.

There is so much relevance to Abominations of Desolation that we will take up this topic in greater detail in the next chapter. For now, remember that discovering within ourselves the source of much of our pain is a pivotal moment in deconstruction, signaling the beginning of our relatively minor role in the process that is bringing us to Jesus and to transformation.

Run Back or Move On? – "Then let those who are in Judea flee to the mountains. Let him who is on the housetop not go down to take anything out of his house. And let him who is in the field not go back to get his clothes" (vv 16–18).

When I finally experience this revelation, I don't feel relief.

Every time I get here, I want to run from it, or cover it up so that no one else will see. If someone else has seen it, which anyone close by will do, I feel humiliated, ashamed, and stricken with an unknown fear, and I want to pull away from them. God knows this is what will happen because He warns that when we feel like running, we should run to the mountain of Judah—to Jesus, as we noted earlier—not back to take anything from our house or to get our clothes. The impulse to run to the familiar is itself a clue that we're about to discover something new; it is another defining moment. So what are we going to run to? There will be a temptation to retreat back to our old ways, our old comfort zones, our security blankets of the past, such as denial, addictive behaviors, depression, unhealthy relationships or damaging thought patterns.

This is exactly what the Israelites wanted to do, when, after having just escaped the clutches of four hundred years of Egyptian slavery, they came to the Red Sea and found themselves blocked in by the advancing Egyptian army. They said,

> Because there were no graves in Egypt, have you taken us away to die in the wilderness? Why have you so dealt with us, to bring us up out of Egypt? Is this not the word that we told you in Egypt, saying, "Let us alone that we may serve the Egyptians?" For it would have been better for us to serve the Egyptians than that we should die in the wilderness. [23]

In Egypt they were crying out in agony for deliverance, but as soon as the rescue mission got tough, they claimed to have been better off in their former state. It's understandable because of the impossible thing standing in their way—a *sea!* I love what Moses says: "Stand still and see the salvation of the LORD." Good advice—usually. But then God says, "Why do you cry to me? Tell the children of Israel to *move on.*" Keep moving, even though there's a large body of water standing in our immediate path? I learn from this that the path we are on is the path He has us on and we need to keep moving on it no matter what appears in front of us. As you move on despite your fear of drowning, prepare to see some parting of obstacles, just as their sea parted.

Waiting – "Immediately after the tribulation of those days the sun will be darkened, and the moon will not give its light; the stars will fall from heaven" (vv 29–30).

Unfortunately, seeing the abhorrent thing in yourself doesn't mean the uncertainty is over. In the hours just before morning, there is still a time of darkness before we see all that Jesus has been doing. And we will see many of the deconstructions and removal of abominations of desolation which we have presented to Him for crucifixion long before we see the new building.

I know we'd all like to speed up these waiting periods, to do as comedian Stephen Wright jokes: "I took a course in speed waiting. Now I can wait an hour in only ten minutes." But the more I see of what God does during the silence, the more I am convinced that the wait is an important part of the deconstruction. It teaches us that we're not in control of this process; it is passive in many ways, but the flurry of activity below the conscious level is astounding, even when we cannot detect anything transpiring.

Very often, waiting is nothing more than an outgrowth of the grieving process. We have just suffered a loss. We simply cannot absorb all that must be sorted through at one time and we have no choice but to linger in this space, without—it is hoped—getting stuck there. A powerful effect of what is called the grief process is that experience of "being journeyed" I mentioned earlier. We may not be able to see that anything is happening, but in this last long hallway before we hear "Jesus will see you now," the corridor we mortals call *time*, we find those parts of ourselves we claimed to have surrendered, maybe even truly thought we had, but which were flattened against the wall in the corner, holding their breath, hoping the trial would end before they were discovered. Remainders of griefs gone by will be found in that passageway too, giving us that feeling that we have been here before. If we are not careful, we will piece together a story of hopelessness from these fragments; a story that we will never be free, never get better, never see Jesus.

Waiting is truth serum. My father-in-law knew this. He was in the grocery business for years and was a master at catching shoplifters. On more than one occasion, when he knew someone had stolen something frozen and had hidden it in their clothing, he would simply wait, engaging them in a friendly conversation from which they could not extricate themselves. Eventually they would begin to squirm. Finally, the discomfort of the icy item against their skin would propel them to surrender it and admit their guilt. The mental image of a kid with a popsicle shoved down the front of his pants dancing a little jig as the evidence slowly drips down his leg helps me endure waiting in a whole new way. Sometimes what I perceive as me waiting on God is really God waiting on me.

You Will See – "They will see the Son of Man coming on the clouds of heaven with power and great glory" (v 30).

The end result of all Jesus has been describing is finally seeing the Son of Man coming with power and glory! Suddenly we will see what He has been wanting us to see all along: Him, in us! The promised resurrection of Christ becomes a reality within us.

The resurrection of Jesus is another multi-layered picture. In John's account of Jesus cleansing the temple, this statement is included which is not found in Matthew's account: "Destroy this temple, and in three days I will raise it up." The Jews asked, "It has taken forty-six years to build this temple, and will you raise it up in three days?" The remainder of the paragraph explains that "He was speaking of the temple of His body. Therefore, when He had risen from the dead, His disciples remembered that He had said this to them; and they believed the Scripture and the word which Jesus had said."

In addition to referring to His own body as a temple that will be destroyed and rebuilt in three days, He also knows the physical temple in which He is standing will be destroyed as the true way to God is revealed. That way, of course, is Himself.[24] And, finally, He knows *we* are a temple that will be destroyed and that our rebuilt temple will be Him. His resurrection is paramount in all three scenarios and is the baseline of all spiritual building. Paul says if the resurrection is not true, Christians "are of all men most pitiable." [25] His prophecy and fulfillment of His resurrection became the cornerstone of the disciples' faith in Scripture and in Christ: "When He had risen from the dead, they remembered that He had said this to them ... and believed."

Transformation episodes are cyclical. We will never finish in this life. Over and over, we will come to this place in the recurring process of relinquishing pieces of ourselves. Initially, this *epiphany*, this manifestation of Christ, will be experienced as *emotional freedom* as we finally accept a truth that sets us free from self, *relief* as the tension that has been mounting is released by our surrender, and as an *increasing awareness* of the fruit of the Spirit in our lives—at least until excavation begins again! Eventually, the progressive increase of Jesus in your temple will begin to feel like a close friendship, a comfort when new transition phases begin.

Oswald Chambers addresses the phenomenon of seeing Jesus:

> Being saved and seeing Jesus are not the same thing. Many people who have never seen Jesus have received and share in God's grace. But once you have seen Him, you can never be the same. Other things will not have the appeal they did before. You should always recognize the difference between what you see Jesus to be and what He has done for you. If you see only what He has done for you, your God is not big enough. [26]

Summing Up

This has been a lengthy chapter and I applaud you for hanging in there. To summarize, God's loving relationship with His temples, which always require purification, will include spiritual deconstruction. It is a one-stone-at-a-time proposition, played out through our emotional responses to the struggles of life so that through revelations of discovery and subsequent crucifixion, each stone will be replaced with Jesus Christ.

In Shinedown's song "45," [27] the question is asked about a person contemplating suicide, "Whatever happened to the young man's heart, swallowed by pain as he slowly fell apart?" Falling apart brings us to the end of ourselves and our own resources where we will find the same despair this young man found, struggling alone with feelings "no one knows," and things he has put "in a box high up on the shelf…a piece of a puzzle known as life wrapped in guilt, sealed up tight." There is no one to help: "Everyone's pointing their fingers, condemning me." Satan will always be waiting at the edge of despair with a suggested escape route: "There's no real reason to accept the way things have changed [when you're] staring down the barrel of a 45." This progression of thought can actually make sense when Satan gets a grip on our minds.

When we hit rock-bottom—as our worlds fall apart and the fate of our hearts is up for grabs—it is easy to understand the appeal of Satan's lure that we are truly at the end, and that there is no other way out. Even if we don't contemplate suicide, at some point in our lives all of us will experience unavoidable pain and loss which will threaten to swallow us. It cannot do so if we so much as entertain—through faith, not appearances—the possibilities a spiritual world promises. In this spiritual world—this *real* world—falling apart is merely the moment we show ourselves ready to be escorted through the divine process of transformation, the perilous path of our "soul's high adventure."[28] God is waiting, not at the *edge* of despair, but at its very center, and has declared that we are not abandoned to walk this path to freedom alone:

> Thus says the LORD … "Fear not, for I have redeemed you; I have called you by your name; you are mine. When you pass through the waters, I will be with you; and through the rivers, they shall not overflow you. When you walk through the fire, you shall not be burned, nor shall the flame scorch you. For I am the LORD your God."[29]

6

Men Bring Stones

"Where we had thought to find an abomination, we shall find a god.
Where we had thought to slay another, we shall slay ourselves;
Where we had thought to travel outward,
we shall come to the center of our own existence;
Where we had thought to be alone, we shall be with all the world."

Joseph Campbell
The Power of Myth

Desperation drives us to places we would probably never go on
our own. For one young man, it compelled a frantic journey to
a foreign country to avoid a fatal appointment with his brother,
from whom he had stolen one too many times. It was Jacob's first
time away from home and he knew he would never see his father
again because his brother Esau had plotted to murder him as soon
as their aged father died.

He drove himself furiously during the day, looking over his
shoulder every few minutes for the dust cloud that would mean
Esau's posse was gaining on him. The effort surely kept introspec-
tion to a minimum. But nightfall was different. Did God lend
him the kind of full moon that makes night feel as bright as day?
Perhaps it was a clear, starry night, the kind that properly orders
one's sense of size in the universe, or maybe it was the inky, en-
veloping blackness that turns the scurrying of nocturnal creatures

into ghostly whispers. Whichever it was, Jacob spent those nights utterly and uncharacteristically alone, unable to avoid thinking about how things could have gone so horribly wrong.

If he was like any of us, his first reaction would be to blame someone else. Maybe he blamed the curse of his name. Because he had been born holding on to his twin brother's heel, they had named him "Deceiver." In his mind, Esau deserved everything Jacob had ever done to him, benefiting as he did from two undeserved graces: receiving the inheritance of the firstborn, and being a man's man, their father's favorite. Both of these had fueled Jacob's manipulative leanings, as had his relationship with his like-minded mother. She had comforted him in his sibling rivalry with the message God had given her while she was pregnant: that she would have twins and that the older would serve the younger. Jacob couldn't see how that was going to happen, nor did he want to wait, so he had looked for ways to fulfill that destiny. Dominance over Esau was the entirety of his vision, so when Esau had practically begged Jacob to take his inheritance in exchange for some food, he had seized the opportunity.

His latest victory—stealing his father's blessing intended for Esau—had been his mother's idea. Neither one of them had given a thought to Esau's grief or Isaac's disappointment. Once he was sure the plan was foolproof, he'd gone along with it. The ruse had been touch-and-go for a little while, but his father had finally succumbed to the deception. Jacob was well on his way to securing the future God had promised.

He hadn't counted on his brother's rage. For the first time, he started to wonder if the future he had been maneuvering for himself could happen—would he even live long enough to fulfill that prophecy? He may even die on this journey before Esau could get to him. What if "the older shall serve the younger" was just something his mother had cooked up to placate him? He knew there was also the possibility that he had blown it; he certainly hadn't been able to collect the inheritance before he left. And who knew if he ever would now? Everything that had seemed stable now seemed to hold no place for sure footing.

He should probably just be thankful his mother had overheard his brother's plan. She had been able to talk his father into sending Jacob to her relatives under the guise of finding a wife, so that was where he was headed, but marriage was the last thing on his mind at the moment. Traveling alone in a treacherous land, Jacob was tormented by the demise of his golden future, his lost parents and his wild imaginings of Esau breathing down his neck.

Frequently, the places to which desperation drives us are turning points in our lives. For Jacob, that journey of fear and regret contained what the Greeks call *kairos,* an appointed time or a moment of opportunity. It was not until he saw that his scheming had created a disaster that God came to him in the night—while his head rested on a stone—and made him a promise. Far more than just the promise of safety from—or dominance over—Esau, it was a reiteration of the promise that had been made to Jacob's father and grandfather, a promise of extreme blessing, privilege, and protection, something he was in dire need of at the moment. When he awoke, he felt rejuvenated with the wonder of what had happened. He said, "Surely the Lord is here and I did not know it. How awesome is this place! This is none other than the house of God, and this is the gate of heaven!"

So he set up as a pillar the rock on which he had laid his head during the night and anointed it with oil, as though consecrating an altar, calling the place *Bethel,* or *House of God.* He made a promise in return: if God would bring him home safely, he would return to this spot, and build a proper altar and there offer a tenth of all that God had given him. Bethel was where his relationship with God first began to be mutual.

In the years that followed, his life was anything but easy. He met his match in Laban, his conniving uncle and father-in-law, who cheated him time and time again. Being on the receiving end of deceit and manipulation likely opened Jacob's eyes to a few of his own rotten stones, as such experiences often do. Despite the numerous difficulties he faced, it was apparent to him that God was blessing him. When conditions with Laban escalated to a boiling point that must have felt familiar, God told him to return to Bethel and build the promised altar, reminding him of his distress with Esau and the vows that had been made there decades earlier.

At Bethel, Jacob built the altar and presumably sacrificed something on it. He called the altar itself *El Bethel*, which means *God of the House of God*. Later, God says that this is where Jacob found Him.¹ *El Bethel* was where Jacob truly met God.

Our story is remarkably similar. Desperation over our spiritual state—or perhaps our physical circumstances—drives us to "find" God, and to offer Him what we have—ourselves. At the time, that is nothing more than a pile of rocks and a promise to live for Him. We find out a little later in Jacob's story that a heap of stones is the biblical picture of a covenant.² God accepts those unworthy stones as our covenant with Him; He claims us as His temple. He then leads us on our journey from our Bethel moment, waiting patiently for us to realize that our attempts to run our own lives or clean up the messes we keep generating are only making things worse.

God is not perturbed by our failures, our calamities, or our innovative attempts to run because He is waiting for us at our destination. (Remember Jonah?) Though it may seem that our circumstances have driven us to *Rock Bottom Café*, we are actually being drawn to our *kairos*, our appointed opportunity to draw near to God in a new way. His incredible desire to fulfill the promises He made to us before we were born—those same promises we have been attempting to collect in our own way—draw us not just back to the *House of God*, but back to the *God of the House*.

Most of us can insert our lives into Jacob's story. I know I can. I had been to Bethel and given my life to God. The requirements of ministry meant that the activities of my life revolved around His work. I see now that I was also simultaneously trying to fulfill His promises of peace, joy and love through selfishness and control of my environment, specifically my marriage. Like Jacob, I was guilty of thinking small, applying those promises to the tiny arena of my personal happiness. I also possessed the certainty that my husband's refusal to live up to my fantasy standard was standing between me and my promised happiness, which meant, ultimately, he and others were hurt in my various schemes to obtain what I deserved. And there was a final, ugly event that put me on the run: adultery.

My adultery and all the events leading up to it—marital difficulties, infertility, church conflict, parenting—were little more than the prologue to the real story. They were evidence of my first deconstruction in process, designed to reveal my utter helplessness and turn me to Jesus from the inside out. Only I wasn't ready to go there yet. Though it brought me back to *Bethel* and became a turning point in my life, the ingenious flight I masterminded kept me from my *El Bethel* for at least fifteen years and allowed me to keep my pretense that I was still in control. Little did I know that God was directing the path toward my *kairos* through an extensive re-education of myself and Him, beginning with an understanding of how we are constructed.

Anatomy of a Temple Wall

Shrek's donkey was right: ogres are layered, like onions[3]—and so are we. Proverbs 23.7 tells us that as we think, *so are we*. We are made up of what we think and believe. Every event, perception and response we experience from birth becomes part of our infrastructure and these self-stones are arranged in specific layers, with the qualities and behaviors we see in ourselves and others being supported and fed from the bedrock layer. It is the discovery and subsequent removal of these stones which comprise the deconstruction of Matthew 24.

The bedrock layers are all about identity: who we are and who God is. Our beliefs at this core level comprise our Abominations of Desolation. That is why our primary task, as author Joseph Campbell noted, is to "retreat from the world scene of secondary effects to those causal zones of the psyche where the difficulties really reside, and there to clarify the difficulties, and eradicate them." If we were to diagram the way we are layered, a cross-section of a wall of a person maturing in the area of sexuality, for example, might look like the image in Illustration A.

Illustration A

Each darker stone represents what author Robert Mulholland calls any "point of unlikeness to Christ."[4] Structural integrity in our temples will be found nowhere else because "no other foundation can anyone lay than that which is laid, which is Jesus Christ." Any kind of stone other than one made of Jesus Christ represents a faulty foundation, an insecure basis for further building. Thus, any area of visible *sin* or *bondage* in my life is supported by emotions and beliefs that are ruled by me and my brilliant ideas of the way things are.

Areas of spiritual and emotional *health* are supported by emotions and beliefs ruled by God, which are represented by the lighter bricks. These reflect areas where God has removed—with our permission—our *heart of stone* and replaced it with *a heart of flesh*—not human flesh, but His living Word or *logos*, His essence—Christ. The bedrock layers contain the same questions over and over again for each surface category. In each category, I have to answer the questions of "What do I deserve?" "What do I want?" "Who is God in this area of my life?" When my thinking lines up with God's, when, for example, what I think I deserve agrees with what God thinks I deserve—which is almost always going to be *nothing*—then that stone has become His. Wherever He has been building, the temple wall looks like a well-built fortress. Wherever I am still me, I look like a pile of gravel!

Though each layer is progressively harder to access, positive spiritual elements become embedded in our deep layers because of the passive nature of transformation that God is working deep within us, aided by the increase of our knowledge of Him through the Word, through prayer and other acts of obedience which promote inner growth. This is what David meant when he said, "I have hidden your Word in my heart that I might not sin against you."[5] The "living and powerful" Word of God is working from within, not just through our deliberate efforts to keep His commands. Where the Spirit's fruit is being produced from within, surface areas of our temple wall—the parts of our lives we can see—are vibrant with health and life.

Notice the relationship of the bricks directly above and below one another. You're not going to find Jesus-stones above me-stones because Jesus is not built on you—you are built on Him! Every causal stone cries out for deliverance with "groanings that cannot be uttered,"[6] trapped, as it were, beneath a load of rubble. There are no words because we don't know what the problem is! Perhaps this is why spiritual realities—our deepest thoughts and beliefs—ultimately reflect themselves in behaviors: so that we might see them manifested and find liberation. Even when we see them, it takes a lot of sandblasting (otherwise known as "life") to remove deep beliefs carved into stone.

From a surface perspective, we are all capable of having good traits right next to bad ones and of having positive surface traits that we carry out through our own strength. The issues we find in the lower layers must be settled over and over again under every kind of surface brick, such as finances, relationships, spiritual service, and body image, just to name a few. It is because of these causal zones that Jesus told the disciples, "There will not be one stone left upon another." Our daily struggles and challenges are the setting for the soul journey that will leave no stone unturned, but our disasters are one of the wrecking balls that blast right through the wall!

Growing in Me-ness
I have already mentioned that I resisted the truths my external difficulties were attempting to expose about my internal condition. I never saw past the first couple of layers, and even where rotten stones were found, I believed my circumstances (things outside of me) were responsible and that my responses were justified. Where I did seek to change, I relied on my own strength to make improvements, which always failed in the long run. So I increased in me-ness, which meant more and more defective layers were being added to my temple. Illustration B provides a diagram of what I looked like in the area of sexuality.

Abominations
The very word adultery is so abominable that you might be tempted to identify that massive adultery-boulder as my Abomination

Illustration B

of Desolation, that curious climax of the deconstruction period we found in Matthew 24. Yet the language of Matthew 24 suggests that our Abominations of Desolation are something hidden, something the conscious mind finds too repugnant to face, something that makes us want to run away when we approach discovery of it. It is also the thing standing between us and a manifestation of Jesus.

As we stated in chapter 5, the original use of the phrase "Abomination of Desolation" is found in a prophecy made by Daniel that enemies of the holy covenant would defile the Old Testament sanctuary by bringing something sacrilegious into the temple. This would not be a random desecration. The offensive items would be placed on the altar reserved for sacrifices in a mockery of the holiness of that ritual.[7] The temple of the living God would be turned into a place of worship for the ruler of darkness. Most scholars agree that in 167 BC, such an event occurred. The words "Abomination of Desolation" would instantly recall to the Jewish mind the Greek ruler named Antiochus Epiphanes who had set up an altar to Zeus over the altar of burnt offerings in the Jewish temple, sacrificing a pig and forcing the priests to eat the unclean animal.[8]

This scene of the Abomination of Desolation holds several eye-opening elements. The first is that it is found on an altar. Consider Jacob's two altars at Bethel. The first one was a rock pile offered enthusiastically after a dream with the vague idea that God had been there; it was a crude altar, but God accepted it as a covenant. Sometimes our encounters with God are like Jacob's: we're sure we've been in His presence, but somewhat unsure and perhaps a little fearful at the same time: "'Surely the Lord was here and I did not know it.' He was afraid."[9] Like Jacob, we proceed in faith, but the strength of the relationship is tenuous as we state the conditions of our faith: "If God does this and such, then I will know it was really Him."[10]

Jacob's second altar was an actual altar and the sacrifice of a tenth of his blessings. It was instigated by God as an integral part of a deepening relationship, and it was the site of a true and mutual meeting of the minds between God and Jacob. The difference in the two altars is like the difference between the wedding and the marriage. Just like a temple, an altar is a picture of a relationship.

Altars

In the Old Testament tabernacle, God had designed two altars: the Altar of Incense and the Altar of Burnt Offering. The Altar of Incense was to continually burn a specific recipe of spices—a recipe that was never to be used outside the tabernacle—whose fragrance was pleasing to God. I love the mental image presented in Revelation 8.3–4 of our prayers wafting upward continually with this fragrance. In contrast, the Altar of Burnt Offerings was the central focus of activity on which a variety of offerings were made: the burnt offering (for atonement), the grain and drink offerings (for thanksgiving), the peace offering, and the sin or trespass offering, and many other individual offerings. Most of these involved the death of animals.

The Altar of Incense could be said to represent the joyful, upward reach toward fellowship with God, those moments of communion and friendship we experience with Him, while the Altar of Burnt Offerings represents the inward, sacrificial journey to Him, the *dark night of the soul* through which every believer must pass.

Offerings

The second significance of Daniel's Abomination of Desolation is in the realm of offerings. Over the years, my idea of offerings has grown significantly. For many years, I believed that worship meant "going to church." It could be boring and long and, frankly, sometimes I didn't want to make the effort. It is difficult now to imagine how an offering that included air-conditioning, beautiful singing and the relative ease of confession and prayer for forgiveness could seem burdensome or meaningless, but the problem was that the entirety of my spirituality was encapsulated in this weekly, sterile, unemotional pseudo-offering. My prayers and obedience throughout the week were just as sterile and shallow.

When I viewed the rubble of my marriage and heart in the months after my affair, I had to ponder why my spirituality had not protected me, but questioning that spirituality gradually exposed its deficiencies. It was in the area of offerings that God began first to broaden my view of worship as more than a Sunday pastime. It was to be a way of living. He let that sink in for a while before He drew my attention to the bloody, death-filled scenes of sacrifice in Old Testament worship.

When I learned that the slaughtering process was not just something one watched the priests do (that would be bad enough!), but that the supplicant had to physically place his hands on the head of an innocent animal, kill it, and feel its life draining out for his sins[11]—over and over and over again—I was grateful to be serving God in a different era. Still, I pondered the sheer number of offerings[12] required of His people back then, compared with our comparatively easy forms of worship and service today. I wondered why the God who never changes would want so much from them and so little from me. Something about this disparity worried the edges of my view of worship like a seam coming undone.

The variety of the Old Testament offerings drew me even deeper into this theme. I believe the various sacrifices found in the tabernacle rituals are representative of the fine distinctions God meant for the giver—and us—to recognize within our relationship with Him. There were offerings that symbolized gratitude, reverence, true recognition of the magnitude of sin, humility, reliance, celebration, relationship and more. When it comes to our relationship with God, we're really talking about a kaleidoscopic unfolding of living layers!

Here is just one example: There was a sacrifice called the jealousy offering,[13] in which a man reeling with the suspicion or proof of his wife's adultery had to present an offering before he could take action against her. That accusation could result in serious consequences, so the time and effort involved in this mandatory sacrifice would prevent frivolous or impulsive accusations, and would press a grieving man to quell his first murderous inclination by entering the priest's and God's presence. The jealousy offering was also called "an offering for remembering, for bringing iniquity to remembrance,"[14] and by following the bizarre procedure which accurately assessed her guilt or innocence, the *husband* was released from his *own* iniquity.[15] Comfort. Accountability. Caution. Justice. Protection. All woven into the jealousy offering.

When I think about the subtle nuances in offerings, I remember the time a friend of mine asked her husband to clean out their garage for her birthday. No other gift would be necessary, just this labor of love. Her husband is a great guy who really would have loved to do this for her, but he knew what would be involved and said instead, "Can't I just buy you some earrings?" and, "How about a nice night out on the town?" Like most women, my friend likes earrings and nice nights out, but as we all know, a nice night out on the town is no substitute for not having to climb over an obstacle course to get to the freezer. For her husband, the cost of those gifts that could be bought was significantly less sacrificial than the painful hours spent sorting and cleaning the accumulation in a garage. That is why my friend has so many earrings!

It's not front page news that Christianity requires sacrifice, but what I began to realize is that though we legitimately sacrifice many things, we do it like the sailors on the ship that harbored Jonah, the fugitive from God. Not knowing exactly what was wrong, they tossed all kinds of cargo overboard to appease the god of the tempest before finally finding peace by throwing overboard the root cause of the storm, Jonah himself.[16] We wonder, just as they did, why the storm still rages. It was because God wanted Jonah. No amount of other cargo would appease. Our time, our money, our service, and even our fannies on a pew are not a substitute for *us*.

Jesus wanted the tithing of mint and cumin along with the observance of weightier matters, but if I keep offering only to meet him at "church" with my financial offering or at Starbucks with my "I'm-drinking-coffee-rather-than-beer" offering, our relationship is going to stay casual. He's promising something very radical, adventurous, and most likely painful when He says, "Let's meet on that hot bed of coals." As I'm stuttering out a lame excuse for why I can't make it, He finishes with, "Oh, and by the way, look down." When I do, I see that I'm already standing in hot coals up to my knees and that Jesus has started the party without me, and I begin to understand what Paul meant when he wrote, "We who live are always delivered to death for Jesus' sake, that the life of Jesus may also be manifested in our mortal flesh." [17]

Breaking Through the Walls

As I have mentioned, the daily issues of our lives are the setting for the discovery of worthless stones in the secondary layers. As each is discovered and we make the choice to surrender it to Jesus, our temples start to take shape, albeit slowly, but when the big *identity* stones at the bottom of the pile are fully recognized and released, the change in us is exponential. A big crisis such as adultery is a wrecking ball that exposes core identities, creating an instantaneous *kairos* for which we are usually unprepared. I know I was. As a result, I became a victim to three separate phases of Satan's deceit which kept me from seeing my Abomination of Desolation for many years.

In the year following the great collapse of my marriage, I began to accept that forgiveness was available for even such a sin as adultery, but my pride could hardly bear that I was a person capable of such an atrocity. I must have seen my Abomination of Desolation for a moment, but I rejected the shameful stone—the one labeled ADULTERESS buried deep in the causal zone—because I didn't want to feel like pond scum. Instead, I said to myself, fulfilling the first of Satan's deceptions, "This is *not* who I am. I lived for 29 years without committing adultery. This was just a temporary stumble in my path." Each year that passed without additional adultery wracked up more evidence to support my claim. In order to completely tune out the abomination at the root of my adultery, a thick deposit of depression was necessary, a layer which eventually had to be addressed in order to break through to the causal zone. I was completely unaware that my denial contained the very name of my battle. The battle was over *Who I Am.* Thus began my real struggle with God.

One of the first things that God did in the rebuilding process was to take my focus off "Who I am" and teach me about *the*

I AM. When Moses,[18] Gideon,[19] and Jeremiah[20] responded to a divine task with "I can't, I'm not (fill in the blank) enough." God never said, "Yes, you are; Yes, you can." He always ignored their excuses and said, "**I** Am, and I Am with you. Enough said." Had I truly known what kind of God I served, I would have seen that when I received forgiveness, that adultery-stone had become a for-given-stone, a reflection of the righteousness of Jesus. As a child of God, at my core, that is *Who I Am*. But I didn't know that yet.

As I began to learn of God, to interact with Him in new ways, and to *believe* Him—which is different than believing *in* Him— some foundational stones began to be replaced with Jesus-stones. These were the veiled stones of ignorance, misunderstandings of His Word, and mis-belief. Each one was painfully removed only as I faced deep rotten stones of myself: selfishness, self-righteous-ness, pride in my infallible doctrinal system, distrust of His grace, fear of new paradigms and my one-talent-man perception of God as a harsh taskmaster.[21]

Along the way, there were also many wounded stones to ex-pose to my new understanding of the healing God I served and the manner in which He wished me to relate to others. One such epiphany was that no other human is responsible for my happiness, my security or my relationship with God. Many me-stones had to be chiseled out, but He took them one at a time, implementing His authority over time, location, and serendipitous introductions to teachers in a way that now blows my mind. I found a *kairos* around every corner during this time.

Satan's Plan B

One *kairos* occurred on the beach in Galveston, Texas on a warm October day, where Satan slipped in his audacious and mostly successful Plan B along with the gift God had planned for me in that moment. I was attending a retreat for preacher's wives and one of the speakers had explained how her husband's infidelity had revealed a path to God for both of them. I nodded my head in agreement, feeling—now five or so years past my own infidel-ity—that I knew what she was talking about. I felt no sadness.

At the end of the lecture, she instructed us to go outdoors and spend one-and-a-half hours in stillness with God. I headed for the beach. The moment my feet touched the sand, a torrent of buried grief and regret rose to the surface, and I cried the bitterest tears I had ever cried. For the first time, they were tears for the actual shame of the adultery, as opposed to the losses that had been associated with it.

Surprised by this unexpected eruption of emotion, I climbed out on a jetty so that I felt surrounded by ocean and began to read from a list of scriptures the speaker had given us. Incredibly, they were all about redemption: "beauty for ashes,"[22] restoration of "the years which the locusts had eaten,"[23] and "gladness regarding the days in which I had seen evil."[24] I was filled with a hope I didn't know I didn't have, and I marveled that He seemed to be reaching right into me, into a wounded stone I didn't even know existed, with His personal touch of comfort and healing. Though I had been trying to run away from a realization of deep sorrow and shame, even that path had brought me right into His arms. This was my first *El Bethel* moment ever.

I rejoiced that day on the jetty in the hope that there could be restoration for my adultery-stone, but of course that meant that I had not received restoration yet, "for we do not hope for that which we have seen."[25] As my view of God was changing, a true view of those me-stones threatened to be exposed, so in the following days, as I contemplated the ways redemption might happen, Satan subtly suggested that my ashes would be made beautiful by preventing other women from jumping off this cliff. I thought this was a great idea! I would be like Peter, whom God allowed to be sifted by Satan in order to reveal his self-righteous and misguided stones, and who was instructed to strengthen his brethren when he returned from his failure.[26]

Meanwhile, the second of my two major deconstructions was in progress, as a recognizable conflict was beginning to brew in our third church in ten years. As I described in chapter 3, the events of this one threw our entire family into crisis, into that dark period where we finally found God. Looking back, it is now apparent that He was stripping away all confidence in other people and in churches in order to clear a pathway to Him, increasing the odds that we would run to Him this time. The similarity of the attacks—but even more so the similarity of my internal responses—revealed in me the same abominations that the adultery was just beginning to unveil these five, six, seven years later: who God is to me, who I am in relation to God, what I think God is doing, and what I think I deserve. When the same painful wounds kept surfacing, it slowly started to dawn on me that they might be related.

I have noticed that when God selects a wounded stone for excavation, He orchestrates occasions for me to trip right and left over blatant reminders of my past pain, chipping away at my avoidance mechanisms, such as the one I use when I am nauseated. I lay statue-still and pretend not to notice that something is trying to surface. I used to do this emotionally, too, trying hard not to feel what was clamoring to be felt. I'm convinced that when the door to our tear-soaked grief chamber opens to allow a new loss in, old losses become attached to the new one by a thread as fine as silk but as strong as a steel cable. Somehow we know that these two together, the old and the new sadness, are whispering a secret to us, a secret cure. The secret is that there is a Healer and you didn't know Him in that other grief like you do now—maybe it's time for Him to take another look at it. As my new and old sorrows intertwined in a period of great grief which was transacted in a completely new context (with the *I Am* as I now saw Him), I saw huge layers of rubble being replaced with life-giving stones of Jesus.

Satan's Plan C

As the life within me increased, I did indeed begin to reach out to other women whom I discovered on the precipice of adultery, but my biggest motivator—I now know—was that it might be an antidote to the shame I still carried regarding that unmoved adultery-stone. My self-redemption effort was seriously hindered by the fact that 95 percent of these women jumped anyway. Still negotiating my way around my shameful stone, Satan helped me conclude that my redemption would instead be accomplished through the grueling task of ministering to their broken bodies found on the rocks below.

After several years of doing just that, I encountered the limit of my ability to take comfort in this way. One more friend had fallen upon those rocks and I found myself unexpectedly angry. That anger helped me see that I had been seriously hoodwinked by Satan that day he whispered in my ear: "This is not who you are." His masterful sleight of hand was that by saying this, he was planting a protest against his real charge: "This *is* who you are." I finally realized what I had been failing to see all along: I was already redeemed! I learned that God does not redeem us *through* ministry, but *to* ministry.

The fact is, without Jesus, an adulteress *is* who I am. I am a covenant-breaker with God and my husband, a person who is "unfaith-full;" I *am* pond scum, and my me-stones reflect that belief. But the bigger truth is that because of Christ, that is *not* who I am. That statement, "This is not who I am," was me running in the exact opposite direction of my Abomination of Desolation, looking for any consolation against the truth that I could find. During my second deconstruction, the question of "Who I Am" had been settled and those identity stones replaced by accepting God's view of who I am. I know this because I was experiencing life in those areas. By encouraging me to continue to hold on to the belief that this is not "Who I Am," Satan had cleverly masked the reality that the adultery-stone had long since been replaced. The illusion about that shameful stone was shattered. The result: no more shame.

This, then, is Luther's *"simul justus et peccator."* It is seeing in one moment both realities: the sinner that I am without Christ, and the righteous, redeemed child of God I am with Christ. If I see only one at a time, I vacillate between my attachment to my righteousness one moment (pride) and the realization of the horror of my sin the next moment (shame). Joseph Campbell writes, "These and all other polarities...bind us to fear and hope," noting that in folklore, they are the "clashing rocks that crush the traveler, but between which, the heroes always pass." [27] Lest you think hope is a good foundation on which to stand in the area of righteousness before God, remember that it does no good to hope that my righteousness will improve my standing before God. It will not. We who are in Christ are clothed in *His* righteousness for our identity before God; it is imputed to us as a gift when we submit to Him.[28] As the old hymn says, "My hope is built on nothing less than Jesus' blood and righteousness...all other ground is sinking sand." [29]

It is natural to shy away from the black places within us, but I am less afraid of facing my abominations when I think of them as the nucleus of transformation. Simone Weil says, "Two prisoners whose cells adjoin communicate with each other by knocking on the wall. The wall is the thing which separates them but is also their means of communication. It is the same with us and God. Every separation is a link." Sometimes I temporarily forget that the very thing blocking my joy hides a secret passageway to Him. I am becoming increasingly aware that if I run away from the rendezvous point with Jesus, *I will not see Jesus!*

The Crux of the Matter: Idolatry

There is one more vital component to the matter of sacrifice. An abomination is anything abhorrent or detestable, but the most literal meaning in Scripture includes the idea of idolatry, or false worship of other gods. Remember how the Abomination of Desolation was a perversion of the intended use of the Altar of Burnt Offerings into worship of a false god, or idolatry? Idolatry is not just bowing down to a bronze Buddha, nor is it simply following pursuits that take us away from God. It is *anything* that we use to support ourselves other than God, whatever holds us together, even respectable things like our spouses, our good deeds, our hurts, our view of ourselves, our beliefs. We must examine our connection to everything in our lives in order to learn where our hearts are not supported by God. These are the stones that hinder the building of our temples, and which men bring as an offering to make room for Jesus to build with His love.

Our abominations are resting directly on the altar on which they should be sacrificed, but until we admit what they are and sacrifice each stone, the altar of sacrifice essentially becomes an altar of worship to something other than God. In other words, that stone remains a god. That is why Joseph Campbell could say, "Where we had thought to find an abomination, we will find a god."[30]

Restoration
Finally, we must see the bigger picture. Deconstruction is the flip side of the coin that is God's invitation to a relationship. If we forget this, we will observe the more difficult aspects of that relationship through the lens of resentment, or at the very least, confusion, which is its own peculiar kind of pain.

It is possible to consider this process and conclude that if God doesn't accept your pile of stones as they are and if His intent is to change you, then He doesn't truly love you. We use this line of reasoning on our human relationships all the time. But the reality is that His love for you is so great, and His power to free you from yourself so unique, that to leave you with no way of escape from the stony prison of yourself would be the action that precludes love.

I recently returned to the scripture that had touched my heart all those years ago and was surprised to see that it included building metaphors I had not noticed. In this passage, Isaiah prophesied of Jesus Christ saying,

> The LORD has anointed me to…preach good tidings to the poor…heal the brokenhearted, proclaim liberty to the captives, to comfort all who mourn, to give them beauty for ashes, the oil of joy for mourning, the garment of praise for the spirit of heaviness. [Then] they shall rebuild the old ruins, they shall raise up the former desolations, and they shall repair the ruined cities, the desolations of many generations.[31]

Our Part
As we have traveled this path together, you may have speculated on the bottom line. You may see what God is doing, but need more information on how you practically participate in the pro-

cess. When David said, "Unless the LORD builds the house, they labor in vain who build it,"[32] he touched on the unique relationship between our efforts and God's implementation. In the chapters to come, we will be examining our part in greater detail. But before we do, it is important to keep the proper perspective in mind.

I have heard the comparison between our part of transformation and God's likened to a flea who hitched a ride on an elephant. When they crossed a bridge the flea said, "We really shook that bridge didn't we?" As we move into the next section, it's important to understand how flea-like we really are in the grand scheme of transformation.

Open Your Mind

Participating in the Building Process

This being human is a guest house
Every morning a new arrival.
A joy, a depression, a meanness,
some momentary awareness comes
as an unexpected visitor.
Welcome and entertain them all!
Even if they are a crowd of sorrows,
who violently sweep your house
empty of its furniture,
still treat each guest honorably.
He may be clearing you out for some new delight.
The dark thought, the shame, the malice,
meet them at the door laughing,
and invite them in.
Be grateful for whoever comes,
because each has been sent
as a guide from beyond.

Rumi

7

Do-It-Yourself Detective Kit

*"So you must listen attentively for what you can barely hear
and do not really want to hear..."*

Eric Maisel, *Deep Writing*

In this chapter, we're going to transition from the conceptual perspective of our spiritual lives—the Big Picture—to its appearance from our viewpoint. It is easy to miss opportunities to apply the spiritual truths we know to our daily lives, to see where the proverbial rubber hits the road. I do not believe God has left us as deep in darkness as we often feel. When one opens up to the myriad ways He is trying to communicate, messages suddenly begin to be obvious everywhere!

Several years ago, my sister-in-law Vickie was involved in an automobile accident. The timing could not have been worse: she had just accepted a fantastic new job in a nearby town, and was in the process of selling her house and planning her daughter's wedding in the old town. She did not seem to be seriously injured, but the preliminary examination she received at the hospital revealed a need for further tests. Something terrible, unrelated to the wreck, had been discovered. She had a colloidal cyst in her brain that had been there since birth. If it ruptured, it could kill her instantly.

As she prepared for brain surgery, she struggled with the possibility of her death, with her concerns about the enormous price tag of the surgery, and with the emotional and daily details of the move and the wedding. The weight of the initial crisis of the wreck, which created its own set of issues, was swallowed by the magnitude of the new crisis, which was ultimately outweighed by her gratitude for the gift in disguise. In the way which things so often work out, she made a full recovery, sold her house, and got her daughter married.

Hebrews 12.2 tells us to entertain strangers, for by doing so, some have entertained angels without knowing it. It was a short leap for us to entertain Vickie's wreck as an angel in disguise because the wait time was short and the relationship between the crisis and the blessing was obvious. We can endure tough times with more grace when we understand the reason, but often, we are not given this vision for a long time—if ever. Nevertheless, I believe it is possible to sense God in every event of our lives, to recognize each struggle as the *kairos* it is, even in those times when the leap is long.

Strange Angels

Exactly how God carries out spiritual cleansing and the deconstruction of our temples and how we participate in that process are profound mysteries of grace. In the previous chapters we have pondered the notion that fear, anxiety, deception, feelings of persecution or isolation, and times of upheaval or dryness are indicative of deconstruction periods, as we read in Matthew 24. When we notice that these emotions are present with such great regularity in our lives, it seems obvious that our daily struggles are some of the most persistent tools God uses to deconstruct us. Our first task of building is to learn to consider everything we experience as a probable manifestation of a me-stone that needs to go.

In many ways, these strange angels are like secret trap doors in the labyrinth of our lives. Like Indiana Jones in pursuit of a legendary relic, following the clues wherever they may lead, it is often when he inadvertently leans on an unmarked stone in a fireplace or tunnel that he is tumbled into the real action. It is just like me resolving on Sunday morning to pursue holiness, then totally missing that the frustration of getting the family ready to go somewhere on Monday, my anxiety over the electric bill that arrives on Tuesday, my explosion of anger at my child's disobedience on Wednesday, the distance I feel toward Steve after he leaves a mess in my clean kitchen on Thursday, or the compromising situation in which I find myself on Friday because of my desire to be accepted by my friends are those unmarked stones that will lead me closer to the deeper relationship with Christ I seek.

As C.S Lewis surmises in *The Weight of Glory*, those things I don't like or don't understand—about God or about life—are the very things I should investigate, probe and enter into: "If our religion is something objective, then we must never avert our eyes from those elements in it which seem puzzling or repellent; for it will be precisely the puzzling or the repellent which conceals what we do not yet know and need to know."[1] We must take care that our examination is not for the purpose of changing other people or even the situation, necessarily. My purpose is to explore *my* reaction.

Fortunately, our responses to our struggles function like blue light specials at K-Mart, flashing and beeping to show shoppers which item is on sale. They are like garish billboards for anyone willing to look. Unfortunately, though we are often quite happy to entertain our woes, coddle our emotions, and protect our motives from exposure to harsh, revealing light or mean people who do not sympathize, we are less comfortable with viewing them as messages of a clean sweep in progress.

When Solomon dedicated the newly built temple, he made reference to something called the "plague of each man's heart." We can safely say that these are the Abominations of Desolation we have been discussing. In that prayer, he indicates that the action that would bring relief from *outside* sources of difficulty from which we need deliverance—problems which seem unrelated to our behavior—is to *come to the knowledge of our own specific plague* and confess *those things* to God:

> When there is famine in the land, pestilence or blight or mildew, locusts or grasshoppers; when their enemy besieges them in the

land of their cities; whatever plague or whatever sickness there is; whatever prayer, whatever supplication is made by anyone, or by all Your people Israel, when each one knows the plague of his own heart, and spreads out his hands toward this temple: then hear in heaven Your dwelling place, and forgive, and act, and give to everyone according to all his ways, whose heart You know (for You alone know the hearts of all the sons of men), that they may fear You all the days that they live in the land which You gave to our fathers.[2]

Remember James 4.1: "What causes fights and quarrels among you? Don't they come from your desires that battle within you?" (NIV). Though there may seem to be no discernable connection between our spiritual, physical and emotional famines, pestilence, or enemy attack and "the plagues of our heart," our circumstances nevertheless reflect and reveal those stones. Although it goes against our natural grain, if we have marriage difficulties, enemies who besiege us, problems at work, shortages of money, depression or any other issue, our primary prayer should be the confession of the plagues of *our* hearts, not how God needs to fix all the other people causing our problems. I cannot emphasize enough that my problems began to lessen when I began relinquishing my sinful stones and confessing the plagues of my heart and *stopped blaming everyone else.*

This is why it is so critical to "examine yourselves as to whether you are in the faith. Test yourselves. Do you not know yourselves, that Jesus Christ is in you?"[3] As we examine ourselves, we are looking for Jesus, and all the places within the causal zones where He is not. The path to that insight is often lit by reliable indicators. Consider some of the following angels in disguise.

Anxiety Calmers

Our behaviors—the ones that seem innocent as well as the sinful ones—can be obvious markers of areas that need deconstructing, especially if those closest to us complain about those behaviors on a regular basis. It might be our spending habits, our television-watching patterns, our computer involvement, our eating or drinking proclivities, our dependence on other people, our withdrawal from social contact, or any escapist activity we do to avoid anxiety. Learning to be "rightly in anxiety," as Kierkegaard said, is a primary task of us all. Learning how to calm those anxieties through connection with Christ is vital, especially since He uses those anxieties to get our attention. The fact is, sometimes He doesn't want them calmed.

A friend of mine struggled in his first job as a psychologist. He was not a part of a Christian counseling office and he was not allowed to address his clients' issues from a biblical perspective (or even from a common-sense perspective, apparently!). There was an expectation that he should help one client assuage her persistent feelings of guilt without addressing the obvious source: an extramarital affair. She wanted to know how she could have her affair and not feel guilty. We sometimes have that same expectation. No only do we want to have our cake and eat it too, we want to lick the spatula!

Emotions

Emotions are tricky things. It is not always easy to know what we're feeling or why, but rarely do emotions exist in us without some kind of internal source and some kind of manifestation. This is how it works for me: When something in my life is putting pressure on me, I think of myself as a sponge that is being squeezed. Just like a sponge, I will release whatever is inside of me. My tendency is to focus on the squeezer, to project all my bad feelings on it or their actions, which ramps up my frustration even more. But when I focus on what is coming out of me when I am squeezed by people, deadlines, deep grief, hormones or general frustrations, the quicker I find the stone that needs to go. The emotions are not the part of us that need attention. They are signals to lead us deeper, to the core sources of our pain, sin and struggle. But watch out! Avoiding those things that squeeze us may appear to be a successful tactic for being a better person, but that essentially guarantees that in order to get our attention God will have to bring out the big juicer, which always squeezes out more than we'd like to deal with at one time.

The origins of our emotions and negative personality traits can be difficult to find. They are often deep-seated offenses sustained since childhood, supported by beliefs we have failed to question. Even when we unearth the sources of our issues, we don't always know how to change the impact our lives have had on our lives. This is where Jesus comes in. As we trace our rag-tag bag of daily emotions to our beliefs and challenge them with God's truth, we come to those rotten, wounded or veiled stones, and then, *to the foundation supporting them.* To trace anger to fear, for example, is a monumental accomplishment, but it is only part of the job. When you recognize what your fear says about your ties to God, you are finally in a position to begin excavating a stone.

Recently my husband's job was looking shaky. We had been concerned for a while about the pressure our beautiful house was putting on our budget. College and other debt we had incurred since purchasing the house were putting our finances on thin ice. We decided to sell it and get into something cheaper and easier to get out of quickly if we needed to relocate suddenly. While we were getting it ready to sell, I was very sad. My friends tried to comfort me by pointing out that it was normal to grieve the loss of a home and all the memories of time spent there. That's legitimate; I have comforted others in this same way. But I decided to go deeper this time. I spent a lot of time in quietness about this, asking for insight into the deepest root cause of the pain. Eventually I got my "unveiling." I sensed God teaching me not to hold to things like houses with so tight a grasp. He brought me to a bedrock stone that revealed a distrust of His provision for me. He'd actually been trying to get this message across for years, because we have moved *so* many times, and every time is hard for me. He was asking me *this time,* to trust Him with more than just my words.

He also revealed a stone made up of pride in the ownership of this house, a signal that I had fallen to deriving my worth from something other than Him. Upon confessing these things and renewing my vow to trust only in Him, I immediately felt peace about the sale of the house. We sold it without even putting it on the market and did very well on it. We moved to a small rental property in need of many repairs. I found that none of my usual complaints and desires about my living arrangements troubled me, even though the house had many drawbacks. Steve lost his job six months later, but we were prepared to financially and emotionally weather that storm better than any we ever had before. The security that seemed threatened by selling our house was actually preserved by that decision, but my security in God's promise that He would never leave me has had a far greater impact on me.

Thoughts

If you begin to notice cause and effect, you will see that thinking that seems to be pleasurable—such as fantasizing about romance, sex, vengeance, success, wealth or *anything different than you have*—is often escapism from a needed area of deconstruction, a temporary reprieve given at the expense of long term joy. I'm not talking about the healthy dreams we all need, which can fill us with hope and enthusiasm, and through which God often directs our paths, but about escapist thinking, which is harmful to us. It doesn't have an energizing effect, drawing us into clarity and action, but rather it has an addictive effect, leading us deeper into ineffectiveness and depression. And if this is true for *pleasant* fantasies, it is even more true for the negative stories we make up whenever someone doesn't call, we don't get the job we wanted, or we fail to live up to our expectations of ourselves. These stories of how awful we are do more damage than all other lies, for they strengthen the mortar around the stones that do not believe or trust God.

Escapist thinking is trying to tell you something about yourself. For a couple of years, I had a fantasy of having my own apartment. I was in my 26th year of marriage and had two kids at home. I didn't want a divorce; I just wanted my own place. I imagined how clean it would stay, how organized the closets and drawers would be, how seldom I would need to vacuum, how my stuff would stay where it belonged, how quiet it would be, and how there would be no stuffed fish on the walls. I would visit Steve and the kids often and do some cooking and laundry for them, but then I would leave them to their messes and their snoring and go back to my place for a good night's sleep. Also, in this fantasy I was ten pounds slimmer.

I spent a ridiculous amount of time avoiding my life in this way, despite my efforts to stop thinking about it. The longer it went on, the more dissatisfied I grew. I was teaching the message of this book to our women's class at the time and we all did an exercise in rooting out the legitimate need that undergirds our longings. Those persistent thoughts of an apartment, once examined, revealed that my God-given need for order and stillness were not being met, and that was hindering a growing—also God-given—desire to write. During this process of discovery, I uncovered a belief that Steve was not supportive of my desire to write, but continued investigation eventually revealed that it was I who had failed to validate that desire, not him. All of this was compounded by the belief that I had nothing that belonged solely to me, a thought I had been suppressing because I didn't believe it was Christ-like.

As I began learning to be not only in the *moment* of here and now but the *place* of here and now, both of which I clearly did not want to inhabit, I scrutinized the Apartment Fantasy. I uncovered valid longings struggling to come to life, which resulted in the clarity to tell my family what I needed, the impetus to enroll in college, the unexpected gift of a computer of my own, a decrease in my obsession with order, and an unveiling by God of the idea for this book. As always, there were some selfish stones to be crucified too: perfectionism, desire for control, victim-mentality, and a lack of discipline in creating inner stillness. As I dealt with those, my Apartment Fantasy began to lose its appeal until one day I noticed it had disappeared.

Pain and Illness

The mind-body connection often yields a great deal of insight into the secrets our souls know about us. Medical research has begun to link specific emotions with certain diseases. Author Christine Northrup, M.D. says, "Depression…is a very well documented independent risk factor for heart disease, cancer, and osteoporosis."[4] In addition, "Dozens of medical studies on breast cancer alone [show] that feelings of powerlessness in important relationships and an inability to express the full range of emotions raise the risk of developing breast cancer and lower survival rates from it."[5] The bottom line, according to Northrup, is that "every thought and every perception you have changes the homeostasis of your body."[6] Even emotional mood-swings caused by hormones, she says, are the body's "wisdom." Hormones do not cause the emotions; they simply force them to surface.

Long before emotions make us sick, we experience physical warnings. If we simply isolate and medicate our chronic physical problems rather than tracing them to the emotions we feel and the emotions to the spiritual need at stake, we miss important messengers that lead to healing. Medication, surgery, nutrition or other interventions may be vital, but the link between spirit and body can be a powerful path to pursue. In being healed spiritually, we may find our physical issues healed as well, or better yet, prevented.

Sometimes our physical conditions reflect spiritual ones of the same nature. A friend of mine is positive that the time she woke up with neck pain so intense she could not function for several days was God's picture to her of her spiritual "stiff neck," a phrase He continually used to describe His people's stubbornness. If you're not sure about these connections, ask Him!

During a very difficult season of parenting my teenager, I developed a persistent pain in one of my hips. No real cause could be discovered, but I began to notice that it was more likely to hurt after an intense confrontation with her. As I began to trace the pain to tension in my body, and the tension of my body to the fear in my heart, I was able to use that pain as a reminder that somewhere deep inside, I was not trusting God with my current situation. When the fear was greatest, I could feel it as a heavy, suffocating tightness in my chest and stomach. I would pray for God's perfect love to simply replace my fear, and it often did—immediately and completely. But soon after, thoughts about our situation would reignite the fear deep inside. Almost immediately, my hip would start hurting before I even knew I was feeling afraid. I began to see it as a gift. I could consciously release the tension through yoga, massage or deep breathing, while focusing on releasing the problem into God's care. The way Steve and I dealt with this particular crisis—through a concerted effort to trust God rather than trying to control the events—resulted in the most satisfying resolution of the problem we could have asked for, and I have only rarely experienced pain in my hip since.

Conflict

The rational mind sees conflict with others as the clashing of two forces, one of which is right and one of which is wrong. Naturally, we perceive our position to be the right one. In the realm of spiritual things, however, other forces are at work. For one, Satan loves to get involved and uses smoke and mirrors to confuse our perception. For another, conflict is very often a projection of our unexamined rotten or wounded stones which we have cast onto other people; it is *our* blue K-Mart light flashing over *someone else's* head because we refuse to see it over our own. Consider Romans 2.1: "Therefore you are inexcusable, O man, whoever you are who judge, for in whatever you judge another you condemn yourself; for you who judge practice the same things."

This is not just instruction not to judge; it is a warning that our judgment judges us. Apparently, judging and condemning universally correspond back to our own "stuff." It is human nature to react harshly to those parts of ourselves that we rub up against in other people, especially the parts we haven't yet recognized. Our judgments of others are often an indicator of the exact problem we need to fix! You've probably been amused by someone ranting about a negative trait in others—a trait that you could clearly see dominates the ranter's personality, but which he seems unable to see. If the rant enrages you rather than amuses you, it's probably because you haven't seen this tendency in yourself yet. I believe the reason this happens is so we can learn to recognize our own shortcomings and to extend compassion rather than condemnation.

I experienced this personally a few years ago when our counselor at the time, Rick, asked us to join an eight-week session with a group of three other couples experiencing similar marital issues. There was a man in the group who was always rude to his wife, a gracious and soft-spoken woman. According to him, everything was her fault. He even turned a homework assignment on his contributions to their problem into a diatribe of all that was wrong with her. This man really got on my last nerve. I asked Rick later how he stayed so calm about this man. His response was, "I've found that most of the time the person that drives us the craziest is the one we're the most like. Basically, you spot it, you got it." The blood that rushed to my head and roared in my ears kept me from having to put my hands over my ears, shake my head and sing to block out his words. Seriously, that's what I wanted to do! That reaction alone should have clued me in, but I chose rather to focus on Rick's words "most of the time." It simply wasn't true with me. I was nothing like that man. In our case, Steve *really was* the one with the problems.

Jesus said that the Holy Spirit would convict the world of sin.[7] I always thought that meant as we read Scripture, He would stir in us responses of recognition and repentance. I still believe He does that, but what happened next taught me that He also convicts personally. In an ordinary moment a few days later—I was in the doorway between the patio and the dining room, bringing in dishes from dinner we had eaten outdoors, not thinking about that issue, when suddenly a long scroll unfolded in my mind containing a list—not mental, not really pictorial—a kind of montage of memories—of possibly every time I had cast blame on other people rather than see my own guilt. There was no cajoling, no trying to convince me. My guilt was specific, obvious and could not be debated. It was humiliating. And, as is typical and expected of Holy Spirit convictions, it changed me on that count forever.

Even accusations from our enemies usually have at least a kernel of truth that links to "the plague of our heart." Sometimes, they lead us to the very stone we have been looking for. What a gift God has given us! A ready-made system for short-circuiting our deceptive hearts. Let me be clear that it's not simply *observa-*

tion of these things in others that convicts us, but the extreme emotional response we experience. I have found—if I am very honest—that even that person who gets on *everybody's* nerves is reflecting a trait of which I am guilty. And when I deal with that thing in myself, I am not so grated by it in that person.

Conflict also has the power to expose deep-seated issues which seem unrelated. Current difficulties to which we overreact are often present in our lives in order to activate similar, unhealed wounds someone else inflicted long ago—so that they can be healed! Because words of affirmation are my "love language."[8] I am ultra-sensitive to harsh words, but I hated the way I reacted so abruptly to even something as minor as an irritated tone. That reaction, once investigated, became a trap-door to the memories of five or six people in my life whose painful words to me had resonated forward to the present, interacting with and complicating new conversations.

The most painful of these had been a verbal beating I received about my adultery in public from someone close to me a year after my affair was ended, while I was still drowning in my own grief and Steve had just begun his. Everything my accuser said was true and I believed I deserved such treatment; for many years her words subconsciously haunted me, and my relationship with her suffered. It took me 16 years to see that I had not, and could not, forgive her because *I had not admitted there was anything to forgive.* My negative feelings for her and my sensitivity to unkind words in general were tied in part to this moment and what I believed about it. Forgiveness came quickly when I stopped suppressing my pain and admitted that she had acted unlovingly and un-Christlike, and that I had been hurt by it. The more I worked on forgiveness in all my verbal wounds, the more my sensitivity to conversational tones decreased.

Finally, it is especially important to notice *patterns* of conflict. If you keep having painful interactions with a certain personality type or you persistently hear certain criticisms about yourself, pay attention to what is coming out of you. Therein lies the stone that needs to go.

Unforgiveness

While they could fit under the categories of thoughts or emotions, shame, guilt and the difficulties of accepting and extending forgiveness are such major roadblocks for many Christians that they deserve a little extra attention. It is not uncommon to hear believers associating sin with its consequences so coldly that they feel and express no concern for those who must lie in the proverbial beds they have made, *especially* if they tried to warn the person. A lack of compassion for those who have fallen into a pit, whether it is toward ourselves or someone else—is a barrier to temple building.

Many people wage this war against themselves, even without outside encouragement, beating themselves up for their failures or discounting suffering that they believe they deserve. Whether we brought the wounds into our lives or not, Jesus showed us that sinners and sufferers of all kinds are worthy of compassion when He said in reference to the woman caught in adultery, "Let he who is without sin cast the first stone."[9] Enough of this insanity! Where there is suffering, our own or another's, there is a need for compassion. Compassion does not equal approval of sin! To say "I shouldn't feel this way," guarantees that you will continue to feel that way, rather than heal and move on. Suppression of feelings only allows them to build up pressure inside us. By the same token, regret and remorse are poor substitutes for forgiveness and healing. To say, "I must feel this way forever," is to play the naked Emperor, parading shame, forgetting that we wear the clothing of the righteousness of Jesus.

My efforts to accept forgiveness and healing were interpreted by my husband, in the early days, as a lack of remorse for my unfaithfulness, but I felt sure that unrelenting remorse would only keep us both in bondage, because it denied the power of the blood of Jesus. I am so thankful that one of the miracles of being transformed is the inexplicable way removal of rotten stones somehow also carries away regret, little by little, making us "free indeed."[10]

If you know someone suffering the consequence of sin or bad choices, perhaps you "ought rather to forgive and comfort him, lest perhaps such a one be swallowed up with too much sorrow." [11] And do not let others' inability to forgive you keep you from forgiving yourself and accepting the forgiveness of God.

Marriage

In his book *Passionate Marriage*, Schnarch describes marriage as a "people-growing machine." [12] He explains that the difficulties of marriage are predictable responses with consistent solutions, and that the very issues that seem to gridlock a relationship are both the cause and the key to the solution. Self-development is at once the purpose *and the tool* for unlocking marital mysteries. (I would add that self-development *through Christ*—or "Christ-development in me"—fulfills this dual role with the added bonus of the power of the Holy Spirit.) I include marriage for two reasons. First, this model of marriage is a smaller-scale version of the process of transformation in life, in general. The experiences of life are designed to bring to the surface those areas that are in need of transformation.

Second, the process of personal transformation is turbo-charged by marriage. Schnarch says, "The task of marriage seems to be finding out who you really are—while fending off someone who's all too ready to tell you!" [13] If you are married, you have entered into a laboratory of sorts in which you will eventually find all your issues dissected under a microscope far more efficiently ("elegantly," says Schnarch) than in any other relationship. I imagine God's original intent was that love would provide a safe environment for the revelation and deconstruction of ourselves as well as a reward for the painful growth marriage requires.

I remember a couple of times in the early years when Steve was evasive with exact truth because he thought it would be unpleasant for me (and thus for him!). Because I believed we were both operating under the principle of "speaking the truth in love," I felt disappointed and discouraged that such a basic tenet was missing in our relationship, as if this were some kind of setback. The thing I must continually remind myself is that a crumbling section of concrete has been there all along, failing to support the house we are building; it's not a new development. The *discovery* is just the opposite of a setback. It's a milestone! A "so *this* is what's been wrong" kind of "aha" moment. An opportunity to make repairs where they really count. Along these lines, psychologist and psychotherapist Eugene Gendlin insightfully said, "What is true is already so. Owning up to it doesn't make it worse. Not being open about it doesn't make it go away. And because it's true, it is what is there to be interacted with. Anything untrue isn't there to be lived. People can stand what is true, for they are already enduring it."

Temptation

If you think about it, you already know that temptation reveals something about you, something shameful of which you are probably aware. But as with emotions, there is a trail to be followed to get to the deepest revelation of our temptation. Resisting temptation is a good thing, especially when we call on the strength of Christ as our source of denial, but if temptation is the result of being drawn away by our own lusts,[14] it becomes the perfect opportunity to explore the basis of our lusts.

To learn what it is that draws us in this direction can make temptation a powerful angel in disguise. Rather than saying, "God, turn your back. I'm going to do this thing," we can face the forbidden thing with Jesus by our side, which is like watching an R-rated movie with your mother or your small child, or like placing mica—fool's gold—alongside a real gold nugget. Beside the genuine, the counterfeit doesn't look so shiny, the hidden snare is revealed and most of all, the blood supply to the appeal is cut off. We simply begin to lose interest.

Had I looked closely into my attraction to an illicit relationship this way, Jesus would surely have pointed out to me the sense of entitlement I had to my own happiness, my unrealistic expectations of marriage, my dependence on others to soothe my self-image issues, my complete unawareness of His desire to have a relationship with me. Addressing these, rather than relying solely on willpower, would most likely have averted this disastrous event in my life because I would have eventually come to the core problem. Author and minister Chris Seidman says, "At the heart of every temptation is the question, 'Can I trust that whatever God asks me to do or not do is based in His highest concern for my well being?'" In other words, who is God to me in the area of this temptation? Is He good, faithful and protective, or is He holding out on me? This is not only key in resisting the temptation, it is a trap-door right to an identity stone.

Grief

"The eye is always caught by light, but shadows have more to say," wrote Gregory Maguire.[15] The shadow cast by grief—that emotional roller coaster ride that transports us from the shock of something horrific to a place of acceptance—is full of angels in disguise. The series of reactions generally labeled as the grief process seem to me to actually be efforts to *resist* the grief. These elements of denial, anger, blame, and bargaining are how our minds gradually receive increasingly greater amounts of truth regarding a loss. I have begun to consider that when these elements are present in everyday events, perhaps a loss or trauma has occurred that we have not identified.

It doesn't have to be a death or terrible catastrophe to constitute a loss. We routinely experience losses throughout our lives, sometimes on an hourly basis! And losses often escape notice as such. I have seen people reach a state of acceptance with the most horrible losses, while others fail, year in and year out, to recover from even little ones. This is often seen in our inability to forgive, which is nothing more than failing to reach the acceptance stage in a grief caused by wounds inflicted by others. When you find yourself pointing a finger, angry, making deals with God or experiencing sadness, ask yourself, "What have I lost?" Be willing to follow that awareness all the way to its hidden stone.

The "loss" of my house taught me that all grief should be examined, for it exposed what I held dear and why. This examination may reveal legitimate and healthy bonds. In that case, our task is to allow ourselves to grieve as we present ourselves to Jesus for healing in order that we might avoid creating wounded stones in our temple. Jesus said, "Blessed are they that mourn." The ability to grieve is actually a gift. Those who allow themselves to mourn in the presence of God will ultimately find the blessing of healing, even when the association is revealed as an unhealthy tie or a substitute for trusting God.

Loneliness

One of my firm beliefs through the years is that loneliness indicated failings on the part of the church or family or friends. If I felt abandoned and alone, it was their fault; they should be surrounding and supporting me. Though I had noticed the phenomenon in Scripture of great men of God undergoing a desert experience in preparation for ministry (Moses, John the Baptist—even Jesus), I hadn't really thought about the loneliness aspect of a desert experience.

Ender's Game,[16] a novel by Orson Scott Card, illustrated a powerful purpose of loneliness for me. The book is set in the future and the earth has been attacked by aliens. Leaders of earth are searching for the perfect child to train to save Earth from the next attack. Siblings Peter and Valentine Wiggin are both brilliant and have been considered, but he is considered too ruthless, while she is too compassionate. So, despite the rules of the culture, their parents are asked to have a third child who might prove to be the perfect balance. Thus Ender is born and at age five, is chosen to save the world.

Ender is put through rigorous training in a school stationed in space. He is intentionally cast into situations that turn others against him. The reader is saddened by the isolation, loneliness, and apparent cruelty and indifference of his trainers that this small boy experiences. About five years into his training, his trainers sense he has almost been pushed beyond the point of caring enough about Earth to want to save it, so they arrange for a visit with Valentine to reestablish a sense of connection and caring in order to give purpose to his task and training. Card does an excellent job of showing in this scene the delicate balance between independence and interdependence necessary in leadership (and life!).

Near the end of the story, the reader learns that although Ender has no knowledge of it, he is deeply loved by his superiors. He has excelled in every area necessary to save the world and passes all the tests put before him with flying colors. His faith in the greater purpose he served enabled him to endure and learn the lessons of loneliness that were required for the job.

Although there are some differences, the similarities I saw between Ender's training and our own lives, especially in ministry, brought me to an epiphany. I realized that loneliness is a tool that God sometimes uses to create leaders who are dependent on Him. Sometimes He runs interference between us and the voices of even well-intentioned Christians so we can hear Him and only Him. Recall that Jesus' final hours were spent not only in agony, but also in loneliness as His closest friends could not even stay awake to pray for Him as He suffered. Deep in the garden, Jesus wrestled with God about the task before Him. He asked God to release Him from the suffering He was about to endure.[17] After the final prayer, everything changed. He came out and said, "Let's do it." Something happened in that time with God, something no person could have done for Jesus.

I am convinced that our transformation *will* include periods of loneliness, during which God is at work, loving us but knowing that something we must learn cannot be learned while we lean on another human being. It is during those times that we may need to do some wrestling with God. We can see from the stories of Jacob, who physically wrestled with an angel of the Lord,[18] and Job who verbally wrestled with Him,[19] that God is up to the challenge and seems always ready to bless His opponent at the end of the struggle.

Crisis

Of course, temptation, marriage, grief, conflict and, for many of us, our daily emotional landscape, all frequently fall into what we experience as crisis, but a real crisis—the kind that causes others to sit up and take notice—is a trap door we have no option of choosing or avoiding. My entire extended family is currently undergoing such a crisis: the loss of our life savings through an investment scheme, and the resulting legal ramifications. This is a very serious situation, yet in the first few weeks I found myself, along with others in my family, occasionally feeling unperturbed and even joyful. This is because our stones in the area of finances are in pretty good shape. We have never had much money, so we have never been able to rely on material things for security. Yet as the reality trickled inward, pockets of fear and dismay began to fill up with the bitter truth, and I began to discover how deeply I really do trust God when, as David said in Psalm 11.3, "The foundations are destroyed."

Though stones of fear are being exposed, my emotional response to truly losing my house—this time it's the equity we had invested, rather than the actual building—is far less tumultuous than the loss I felt over selling it. Daily, I recall how the former crises of my life taught me so much about myself and Him that I could never have learned any other way. As He has repeatedly drawn my attention to His faithful provision before, during and after each calamity, my faith and trust have been built to the point where I have spent very little time trying to figure out how we will survive this catastrophe. Instead, I concentrate my energy on learning to wait patiently for His redemption of the situation while I allow Him to excavate all the me-stones that are revealed through this crisis. Like all difficulties, this is really another *identity* crisis.

As William P. Young says, "Faith does not grow in the house of certainty."[20] The Holy Temple we are becoming is at every moment exactly what Jesus is building, but for us, this will very often feel like a house of *uncertainty*. Not only will our faith grow as we watch God work out situations in ways we could not imagine, but we will see how who we are and who we want to be line up with each other. What is already known in heaven will become visible on earth. This is the power of crisis.

The Most Comforting Angel of All

Of all the unexpected gifts we receive, one of the most enlightening is learning that every personal struggle reflects a legitimate need that God has promised to meet. This bears repeating: our mental, emotional and many of our physical issues all stem from our misplaced efforts to meet *legitimate* needs. When you experience pain or temptation, you are as close as you can *consciously* be to discovering both the legitimate need and the part of your identity He is asking you to hand over to be put to death. There's always something to crucify, followed by a powerful resurrection of Christ in that place. There He will show us how to let Him meet those deepest inner needs so that our relationships will not be taxed by our insatiable desires, but will instead be reflections of His love.

What if we could look at these endless, daily events as the conflict element of our stories, the perils the hero faces which puzzle and confuse him, but which serve as the challenge that reveals his inner strength—as well as the parts of him that need to be surrendered—as they lead him to the pinnacle of his soul's adventure? I am convinced that this is not a fairy tale, but reality. As G.K. Chesterton wrote, "An adventure is an inconvenience rightly considered." [21]

If we thought of our struggles as the challenge of being squeezed by forces ultimately working for our good, we would feel less inclined to run away, as Bebo Norman contemplates in his song "Disappear." His inclination to disappear by running away from the world is rechanneled when he catches the lie and remembers that the only way to get away from himself is to disappear into Christ. Then the things that squeeze will reveal not himself, but Jesus and love.

> On a day like this I want to crawl beneath a rock
> A million miles from the world, the noise, the commotion
> That never seems to stop
>
> And on a day like this I want to run away from the routine
> Run away from the daily grind
> That can suck the life right out of me
>
> I know of only one place I can run to...

> I don't want to care about earthly things
> Be caught up in all the lies that trick my eyes
> They say it's all about me
> I'm so tired of it being about me...
>
> I want to hide in You
> The Way, the Life, the Truth
> So I can disappear.
> And love is all there is to see
> Coming out of me
> And You become clear
> As I disappear.

Unfortunately, it often takes the daily grind sucking the life right out of us to desire to hide in Christ, to long for the diminishment of ourselves and the revelation of Christ. We need that squeezing to help us identify the contents of our hearts so that eventually all the squeezing reveals only and clearly Christ, only and clearly Love.

Still, there are days when motivation to make the difficult effort toward discovery is hard to find, especially when there is an easy, non-sinful "anxiety calmer" that can do the trick, or when our lives seem to be running along moderately well. Sometimes it is helpful to rest from self-discovery, but there are several reasons not to wait until we are forced.

First, Jesus came to give us abundant life,[22] not mediocrity. "Mostly okay" is a far cry from abundant living. Joy, peace and creativity (all three of which are expressions of love) are the living streams that flow out of the fountain of the Lord, yet we often try to function from the strength of broken cisterns that can hold no water.[23] In other words, we settle.

Second, you may have heard the old wives' saying "a stitch in time saves nine," meaning that if we tend to things while they are manageable, we will not have to tend to them in more painful ways later. It is easy to turn off the intuitive awareness we have of subtle disharmony brewing somewhere or of reckonings ahead. Sometimes the sheer constancy of these signals and the helplessness we feel convince us that our very sanity is dependent on disconnecting, tuning-out and medicating. This avoidance will require a full-scale earthquake to awaken us, and when it comes, we will most certainly not be ready. Earthquakes will happen, but when our bedrocks are in place, they will often register only as tremors.

A Pebble in Your Shoe

It's time we started connecting our daily lives with the realities of being a temple. One of the easiest ways to make those connections on a daily basis is paying attention to feelings of irritation, annoyance, anger, sadness or anxiety. These emotions that may seem trivial are like pieces of a stone that have broken off during Jesus' excavation efforts and worked their way into our shoes, projecting themselves into our consciousness. We can keep hobbling along or kicking them out, cursing their existence, but another pesky pebble will appear in our footwear until we realize there's a boulder with our name on it that needs some work. Far better to cooperate with the work going on in the quarry!

8

Defining Moments

"What power had I before I learned to yield?
Shatter me, great wind: I shall possess the field."

Richard Wilbur, *To a Milkweed*

Several years ago my friends Deondra and Justin went bungee jumping. They stood on a solid platform seven stories high for several long moments, trembling, summoning the courage to step off. Their motivations for this undertaking differed: facing and overcoming fear was the primary motivation for Justin; Deondra was in it for the exhilaration. She had been skydiving the year before, but was surprisingly just as nervous about the jump as Justin. Though the anxious moments before the jump dominated the conversation later, the descent provided both of them with a thrilling feeling of freedom and a sense of empowerment at the courage they had shown, just as they hoped it would. I had gone along to capture the moment on film, and concluded that nothing says "defining moment" as patently as bungee jumping.

In contrast, when I saw Justin's next adventure, a free fall from 16 stories, I recognized another common—yet completely different—kind of defining moment. In this plunge, he was strapped into a harness suspended 16 stories above a net. Justin asked the operator to release him on the count of three. He started counting: "one—" and then he let Justin fall. The surprise of falling before he was ready threw him off guard and caused him to miss out on the adrenaline rush he was expecting. Losing that moment in which to prepare for the short thrill thrust him into a state of alarm which quickly turned to anger. His expectations had been thwarted; he had not received the effect to which he felt his $30 entitled him, and the small amount of control available to him had been stolen. He walked away from the experience feeling frustrated, rather than exhilarated.

The Privilege of Choice

If you will recall, the discovery of the Abomination of Desolation in Matthew 24 was not the end of the deconstruction period. After that came a defining moment—a point of decision addressed by the warning not to run back to old securities, but to run instead to the mountain, which we identified as Jesus. There would be more darkness and earthquakes and a time of waiting, but if they endured, they would finally see the Son of Man coming in glory. They would only see Jesus if they *chose* that which represented Jesus (the mountain) when the inclination to run came over them.

Defining moments are so-called because they define the direction we face, the action we take, the person we are becoming. We are presented with a choice, a decision is demanded, and we know our response will define us. We are fortunate when the moment and our options are obvious, as though a marquis with flashing lights is announcing the magnitude of the moment and shining a spotlight on our brave decision to step off the platform while a drum roll builds anticipation of the climactic moment, as with Justin and Deondra's bungee jumping experience. Though the decision may be difficult, when the choices and the ramifications of each seem clear, we are on full alert, empowered with the privilege of choice.

As Justin's second fall illustrates, however, sometimes we do not appear to have a choice in the events that shape our lives—the breakers of life hit us unexpectedly from behind when we turn to show someone the starfish we have just found. For a few moments, we are plunged into a torrent of chaos, not unlike laundry in a washing machine, with no perception of up or down. The immediate crisis ends, leaving us bedraggled, spewing salt water, and wondering where our bathing suit is. In life, we will sometimes encounter disappointed bystanders who feel we should have handled that hit more gracefully or rebuke us for wading out so far. We may even feel that way about it ourselves. But that calamity was not the defining moment, and our initial reactions are often outside our control (except as our growing transformations change us from within).

The seeds of our defining moment are being planted as the water recedes. We didn't choose to get knocked over by a killer wave, but the immediate and frenetic effort of our minds to make sense of what happened is where our choice begins. Are we going to be angry at God for creating the ocean and never visit it again? Are seeds of bitterness going to be planted in our hearts toward those disapproving onlookers? Are we going to berate ourselves mercilessly for allowing ourselves to be caught off-guard? Our responses to our "drops" may have even more an impact in defining us than the decisive moments when we choose to jump, partially because there is no drum roll or spotlight to alert us to the importance of the decision.

This kind of defining moment often passes by unnoticed. We realize only in retrospect that we have missed a critical opportunity and are currently being defined by default. Or we may have agonized over the choices without the ability to know the far-reaching implications a seemingly insignificant choice would have, and discovered that we made the wrong choice. But it is never too late! There is always another opportunity to choose. The act of awakening creates a new defining moment.

Not Choosing

Some people have more difficulty waking up in the morning than others. Sometimes it's because they stayed up late too many nights in a row, or maybe they're just not morning people. Maybe they dread the task that must be faced that day. For these souls, getting up is less than energetic, and they put it off as long as possible by multiple hits to the snooze button.

Sometimes we hit the snooze button on our defining moments by stalling, misdirecting, rationalizing or feigning innocence. Perhaps we fool ourselves into believing we have forged a new path at the fork in the road or that we are merely pausing at the intersection, contemplating our options. Both of these actions blind us to the fact that we have already made a choice to take the road of self-preservation. This is equivalent to *Clean Sweep* participants hugging a box of useless odds and ends to their chests, justifying the space it will take up in their "temple," denying the harm it causes, or possibly even admitting it is worthless but crying that they can't let go of it.

Perhaps we claim that none of our choices will do, so we refuse to make one, seeking compulsory solutions, even though we *hate* not having choices. I observed this once at a family reunion. Two young girls were playing a game in which they intended to slap each other's hands until one of them cried "uncle." Eventually, one of them cried "uncle" in another way by turning to the grownups watching and saying, "Would one of you please be an adult and make us stop?" She correctly assessed her dilemma in the hand-slapping game as childish.

The real immaturity was in acknowledging only two choices: lose or keep playing. She thought submission meant weakness and defeat. Her limited view of surrender carried with it only negative connotations of the word: give in, give up, capitulate, admit defeat, submit, relinquish, yield, resign, bow out, abandon ship—words and concepts that do not represent the portrait of strength or victory with which both she and her cousin wished to be identified. She had bought into the prevailing idea that if somebody wins, somebody else has to lose, and that the world's idea of losing is accurate. She felt trapped by the choice of two pains: the painful *idea* of losing, or the *actual* pain of staying in the game, unable to reconcile her desire to quit with her paradigms about success.

The adults nearby could clearly see another choice—and perhaps this is the growing mark of maturity: our ability to recognize that surrender is an act of courage, wisdom and intelligence, not cowardice and weakness. If this girl had been able to see that surrender in this case would actually be a win, her pain would have ceased. Because of our uninvestigated definitions, we sometimes find ourselves in the position that Emerson Hart's song "Ordinary" ponders: "How did I become responsible without ever taking responsibility?"[1] We might have gotten there by being pushed, but most often our refusal to make a decision about how to respond is a decision in itself.

Anaïs Nin said, "There came a time when the risk to remain tight in the bud was more painful than the risk it took to blossom." Being forced to choose between two pains is excruciating, but we are often brought to this brink because of our refusal to make necessary changes until the rotten stone is causing us greater pain than our fear of relinquishing it. I will admit that this is my primary motivation for change. I readily identify with Daffy Duck who said, "I'm not like other people. I can't stand pain; it hurts me."[2] This is perhaps the only time in my life I would prefer not to have a choice; I'd like Jesus to just force the stone from me. But it is not surrender if the decision is not ours. There is no resurrection if a crucifixion doesn't take place. Jesus wants no less from us than He demanded of Himself: "No one takes [my life] from Me, but I lay it down of Myself."[3]

There are two things we face: the *dilemma*—the difficulty of making the choice; and the *cost*—the difficulty of living out the choice we have made. In the context of transformation, at least, we rarely face the dilemma of what to choose. When we truly see the rotten stone, the awful realization cannot be avoided: we know it needs to go. But we *are* faced with the difficulty of the choice. *How* do we let go of a part of ourselves? How do we survive the *pain* of surrender?

Questionings
These are reasonable questions. Elie Wiesel, a holocaust survivor who wrote the book *Night*, says, "Man comes closer to God

through the questions he asks Him."[4] He believed there is a power in questions that does not lie in the answer. This is why God saw fit to include for our consideration even the most accusatory questions David threw at Him. Each Psalm contains a microcosm of David's soul-journey and illustrates an ineffable transference from questionings to satisfaction and praise.

Our problem is that we ask our questions and then never put ourselves in a position to hear the answers. We ask, "God, why won't you answer?" and then we turn on the television, the computer, and our mp3 player, then we pick up the phone and call a friend while we chat online with another one. We will never hear His whispered answers in such chaos. Likewise, we will miss His answers if we never pick up a Bible or if we cling to our preconceived ideas of the specific manner in which we expect to hear from Him—such as giving us what we want.

If you study the way God and Jesus answered the questions posed to them in Scripture, you will see that they always drew attention away from the human perspective to a higher plane, rather than just answering the question. Though I try to offer this perspective to people who are struggling, I am amazed at how often they don't even want to *try* to make this shift.

I have had my own difficulties with that transferal. How long did I wait for answers that never came in a verbal or cogent form before I made the movement of surrender? Sometimes quite awhile. Though I searched the Scriptures, my rational mind had difficulty with the paradoxical concept of self-crucifixion, yet when I finally did it, the mysterious effects of surrender had a way of making "I AM" a perfectly acceptable reply to my question of "Why?" I was so surprised to arrive *through surrender* at a peace that "surpassed understanding,"[5] a calm that became all the answer I needed, a place where my *why* evolved from "Why is this happening to me?" to "Why do You love me so much?" My belief that control brings security was shattered when I stopped withholding my action pending God's answers and discovered via obedience that surrender brings peace. I began to realize that my attempts to demystify this miraculous gift were the problem, not God and His mysteries.

Ask your questions; it's not like God hasn't heard them all before. Just be sure to give Him the opportunity to answer in all the ways He chooses. Very often, the channel of surrender itself is one of the vehicles for His answers to find their way to us.

Trading Spaces

The story of Justin and Deondra bungee jumping reflects a healthy approach to surrender. Whether our leaps hold the visible promise of joy as was the case with Deondra, or they embody a wrestling match with God, similar to Justin's fear—it is in our best interest to evaluate our rationales and uninvestigated motives for either jumping, or duct-taping our feet to the platform. Like Justin and Deondra, we have to focus singularly on and believe wholeheart-edly in what we will gain in order to overcome the painful idea of jumping.

As I talked to Justin and Deondra about their gravity-defying experience, I found myself intrigued at how closely their observations mirrored spiritual truths. Reflecting on her jump, Deondra later said, "You can't see the rope, either before the leap or during the fall. It's all about faith." Because *I* could see the bungee cord, I didn't realize that bungee jumpers feel as if they're falling without support. Because their security line is invisible to them, trusting that it was there was paramount. When we make our proverbial leaps of faith, we can't see the ways in which God is supporting us. Faith is choosing to believe that even though we are falling, God is still with us.

When we examine the so-called cost/benefit ratio of cruci-fixion decisions, even good reasons will not overcome the fear, as echoed by Justin's comment, "You can't wait until you're not afraid to jump." In bungee jumping, as in all forms of surrender and crucifixion, our feelings cannot be the deciding factor, because it will never feel pleasant beforehand. At the crossroads of deci-sion, sometimes the only true motivator is our faith that God will make sense of our willingness to choose His way.

Finally, Justin shared that when he stepped off the platform, all he could think was, "'I love Jesus,' while I gave Him the only thing

I had—my trust." The instant we give our full trust to God, fear vanishes and its opponent—love—becomes both our motivator and what we will experience. In the free fall, what is real becomes crystal clear. All former doubts and misgivings are forgotten.

My friends' bungee jumping experience teaches me that it makes no sense to try to let go of something unless we are trading our grasp for something more substantial. If we focus on the thing we must surrender, letting go is agonizing and sometimes seems impossible. Defining moments become victories when our choices are anchored on the trade, on transferring our grasp, not simply letting go into nothingness.

Even when we focus on the trade, our approach to surrender is also a critical factor in victory. A goal-oriented approach to surrender, powered by self-will (Let go! Right now!) can put us in an all-or-nothing state of paralysis. Preferable to that is a process-oriented approach which *examines* the roots of our present choices, *acknowledges* the negative impact our current choice is having on us, *believes* in the value of a particular surrender, *trusts* in the unseen outcome made possible by a power outside ourselves—and then actually *steps off the platform!* Though it sounds more time-intensive, process-oriented surrender can become a very streamlined practice for us, fast-tracking our transformation in a way our efforts to demand self-surrender never will.

Preferring Joy

An excellent parable about transferring our grasp is told in C. S. Lewis' *The Great Divorce*. In this story, inhabitants of hell are given the opportunity to visit heaven and to stay if they wish. They are met by a hand-picked messenger from heaven (someone they knew or admired) to meet with them and convince them to stay, but most do not. The main character is more open-minded to the realities of heaven than most and is given the opportunity to witness several of these conversations. He repeatedly sees that the choice to remain in hell is sealed by their refusal to let go of something:

> "Milton was right," said my Teacher. "The choice of every lost soul can be expressed in the words, 'Better to reign in Hell than

serve in Heaven.' There is always something they insist on keeping, even at the price of misery. There is always something they
prefer to joy—that is, to reality. You see it easily enough in a
spoiled child that would sooner miss its play and its supper than
say it was sorry and be friends. Ye call it the Sulks. But in adult
life it has a hundred fine names—Achilles' wrath and Corio-
lanus' grandeur, Revenge and Injured Merit and Self-Respect
and Tragic Greatness and Proper Pride.

"Then is no one lost through the undignified vices, Sir?
Through mere sensuality?

"Some are, no doubt. The sensualist begins by pursuing a real
pleasure, though a small one. His sin is the less. But the time
comes on when the pleasure becomes less and less and the crav-
ing fiercer and fiercer and though he knows that joy can never
come that way, yet he prefers to joy the mere fondling of unap-
peasable lust and would not have it taken from him. He'd fight
to the death to keep it."[6]

In *The Great Divorce*, the inhabitants of hell suffer from a
strange proclivity to call the sawdust in their mouths water, and
refuse a real drink of water. Even when souls enjoying the wonders of heaven try to convince them to stay, they prefer to hold on
to a far inferior substitute, sometimes out of disbelief, other times
out of pride—always out of deception, much like that found in
Isaiah 44.20: "He feeds on ashes. A deceived heart has turned
him aside. He cannot deliver his soul nor say, 'Is there not a lie in
my right hand?'"

To me, this story is really a parable about life on earth, for we
often act just like these condemned souls. Over and over again,
the point is made that if we will just release "it," we will get "it"
back in a glorified form, whether "it" is maternal love, sexual desire, or the love of good things, such as wisdom or art:

No natural feelings are high or low, holy or unholy, in themselves. They are all holy when God's hand is on the rein. They
all go bad when they set up their own and make themselves into
false gods...every natural love will rise again and live forever in
this country; but none will rise again until it has been buried.[7]

Thus, in Lewis' story, surrender is the defining action that determines both our final destination and the eternal life we are, in a sense, already living. While standing on the threshold of heaven, it seems impossible that people would choose hell, but without fail, anyone clutching an inferior object or notion does so because he does not see that it is inferior, or he does see it but believes the cost or pain of exchanging it to be too high for what he will get in return. He does not know, want, or trust what he will get in return.

Lewis concludes: "In the end there are only two kinds of people: those who say to God 'Thy will be done' and those to whom God says, in the end, 'Thy will be done.'" Always given the choice, we will ultimately be granted our will. We see this dynamic in play with the Israelites. God gave them what they lusted for, but at a cost:

> He rebuked the Red Sea also, and it dried up, so He led them through the depths, as through the wilderness. He saved them from the hand of him who hated them, and redeemed them from the hand of the enemy. The waters covered their enemies; there was not one of them left. Then they believed His words; they sang His praise. They soon forgot His works; they did not wait for His counsel, but lusted exceedingly in the wilderness, and tested God in the desert. And He gave them their request, but sent leanness into their soul.[8]

Being Let Go

We often use the phrase "let go," but author Byron Katie poses the idea that when we examine our beliefs and align them with truth, the surface difficulties we face—the things we think we need to let go of—will let go of us.[9] Second Corinthians 10.4–5 encourages us that in the battle for our flesh, which is waged in our minds, every thought can and must be brought into captivity. Throughout this book, I have made the claim that we should not simply suppress our thoughts, but that they are valuable clues to ourselves and to who Jesus really is to us at any given moment.

The concept of "taking captive" may seem contradictory to the idea of "surrender." They are, in fact, opposites. Consider what happens when a thought has taken *us* captive. I tried to help someone once who could not let go of the thought that his faith and strength were dependent on someone else's behavior changing. As we walked through the logic of this thought, the person agreed that the thought could not possibly be true and was the source of considerable pain, and that not believing this thought would indeed be freeing. Yet at the end of the discourse, the pain and sadness of letting go of the thought overpowered and jerked him back to his original difficulty, which he defended with Scripture about the sinfulness of the other person's behavior. My friend felt more hopeless than ever as he clung to his original belief.

I couldn't help but think about the warning in Matthew 24 about the inevitable desire to retreat to old comfort zones when things start shaking and the Abomination of Desolation is coming in to view. Weeks later, he found a powerful truth to which he could cling, a truth that finally outweighed the lies he had been holding on to. With no further effort on his part, the painful thought let go of him and he made an overnight turnaround in faith, strength and joy. It was just a tiny shift in thinking. There was no dramatic, painful moment of surrender as we usually envision it. The surrender was in the trade and it was so triumphant, no pain was experienced.

Do you remember my Apartment Fantasy? When I understood all that it was masking, and began to hold on to *those things*, the Apartment Fantasy, in the same way, let go of me.

This is an important distinction going back to the layers in our temple walls. Beliefs are held in the lower levels. We hold them. Thoughts are in the upper levels, growing out of those beliefs. They hold us. We have all experienced the dilemma that the more we try not to think of something, the more we think of it. "The truth shall set you free" means we were being held captive by lies at some level. When we turn and take captive our thoughts, interrogating them with the diligence of Jack Bauer, the terrorist-crushing hero of the hit television show *24*,[10] they will lead us to a truth that will either turn those thoughts into non-issues or we will discover, at the belief level, that which we need to crucify.

Perhaps that is why the Bible doesn't tell us to "let go." Instead, nearly every exhortation to *not* do something is followed by the *how*, shifting focus from avoidance to action and showing us how to concentrate our energies where the power is, as in "Set your minds on things *above*,"[11] and "Don't be anxious... think on *these* things" (truth, purity, holiness, etc).[12] In the various contexts where God tells someone not to fear, you will always find a superior focus, such as, "Do not fear, for I am with you."[13]

The Two Faces of Crucifixion

We have been speaking of the Christian's death, deconstruction and crucifixion in fairly general terms. I have tried to bring the concept into the very heart of who we are, and to show how important it is in our transformations. The question that still remains is *how?* When we finally accept the truth that a stone must go, the surrender—the crucifixion—in our defining moment will always be accomplished through one or both of two old-school standbys: *trust* and *obedience.*

Although I was raised singing the simple hymn "Trust and obey, for there's no other way to be happy in Jesus,"[14] I had some very confused ideas about the roles and implementation of these two acts. I was not very good at either one, though I believed that I was. It took me a while to see that the essence of my difficulty with both responses was my tenacious desire for control. Rather than control, both actually represent surrender: trust is surrendering your fear; obedience is surrendering your will.

Trust

As we speak of trust, remember that we are applying it in our defining moments, the points of decision when we have seen our Abomination of Desolation, or any other stone that we know requires crucifixion. Since the me-stones in our causal zones are often based on mis-belief about who we are in Christ or who God is, believing what God says requires faith, because things always look different from an earthly point of view. It is easy to *say* or *think* we have faith and not know that in our deepest layers we do not—until we find ourselves teetering on the edge of a platform.

Trust is the body language of faith. Body language has become a much-studied form of non-verbal communication. Our bodies continually transmit messages that may even contradict what we say. Trust is a tangible link between what we believe and what we do. The body language of anxiety may be a worried look, a nervous habit, an eating binge, or the need for a cigarette. The body language of trust is seen in Isaiah 26.3.

The promise found there is instructional when read in English: "You will keep him in perfect peace whose mind is stayed on you, because he trusts in You." But when I looked up the origins of the words contained there, I was surprised at the physical representations some of the words contain. The word "keep" (Heb: *natsar)* means "to preserve, guard, or keep close, specifically as a watchman." "Perfect" and "peace" are actually translated from the same word *(shalowm)* and together, they mean "complete safety, tranquility, and contentment." The "mind" *(yetser)* signifies "something framed," or one's "purpose or imagination." "Stayed" *(camak)* means "lean, lay, rest." "Trusts" *(batach)* describes the one who "has confidence, boldness, feels secure."

The posture of trust is one of leaning. God preserves and closely guards us when we lean our purposes and imagination on *His* framework within us. This keeps us in a place of safety and tranquility which results in feelings of security and boldness! What I have found is that when my purposes and imagination are framed by me and my ideas, I am not at rest, I have no tranquility. And when I have no tranquility, I am not confident and bold.

When we lean, we are at rest because we truly believe what we are leaning on will support our weight. Imagine leaning against a banister that feels wobbly. You are unlikely to prop yourself against it or hoist yourself up to sit on it. But if it is solid, you will not hesitate to put all your weight on it, or even slide down it

The idea of framework reminds me of that section of a wall in chapter 6. My mind was framed and constructed by my own ideas of who God was and what He was doing, and I was unhappy and ended up in serious trouble. As I began to align my thinking with God's, to *believe what He said* even when it made no earthly sense to me, my framework began changing. The more I leaned on *that* framework and not my own, the more trustworthy it began to feel and the more peace and tranquility I began to experience. I eventually learned that if "all things work together for good" is true, then any instability I feel is about my lack of trust, not an indicator of a wobbly God.

When I think of all the things we lean on for support, I am amazed at how willing we are to do so without investigating the trustworthiness of those supports. Our transformative journeys are, in many ways, nothing more than God allowing those rickety supports of money, relationships, beauty, and health (just to name a few) to collapse under the weight of our troubles. Very often I have believed that God has given way, but I now know my discomfort was really the painful disintegration of my definition of Him, my false expectations of Him, and my misapplication of His promises to my purposes and not His. I was guilty of demanding guarantees He had not promised and refusing to believe the ones He had. And this showed up not only in my trust level, but in my physical health.

All these ideas came together for me during the two years I was sick. My doctor explained that my health issues were the result of chronic stress. He had a reasonable belief that if God truly existed, His people would not become ill from stress because their relationship with Him would alleviate their anxieties. He had seen so many Christians who weren't experiencing peace that he was becoming a reluctant atheist. When he asked me, "Aren't you a Christian? Don't you have prayer as an avenue for dealing with pressure?" I got the picture. Not only was I not sliding down the banister, I was exhibiting a phobia of stairs.

I have mentioned several times how gifted I am at resistance. Resistance reminds me of arm wrestling with all the inherent tension, struggling, straining and grunting. Resistance is war! In a recent bout of resistance, I moved from hurt to anger and was approaching bitterness over the loss of a friend a year earlier. Just as in arm wrestling, remaining in this contest had brought me exhaustion, weakness against further attacks from Satan, and an inability to effectively function in other areas, as all my energies were devoted to managing this struggle. By experience, I could second Simone Weil's insight on resistance: "In struggling against anguish one never produces serenity; the struggle against anguish only produces new forms of anguish."

I was getting tired of the pain. Could surrendering the whole situation to God and forgiving and releasing my friend be more painful than the effect it was having in my life? I realized that even as I was explaining to you the concept that "all things work together for good," I had allowed my belief about this event to fall outside that umbrella. *This* loss could certainly not be used for good! As I questioned whether I truly believed this scripture, I knew that I did and that it was time to apply it to this situation. I decided to trust God to bring good from the loss. To step from the platform and feel the wind in my hair. To cling to and rest on His promises rather than my desire.

I was thankful for this experience at the time of the writing of this chapter because it reminded me how difficult it is to surrender and choose trust. I was humbled by how easy it is to miss a defining moment, and to say to God, "No, this one is not part of your promise about 'all things.'" This temporary setback prompted me to emphasize again that we are in a *process*, and to remember all over again the steps necessary to choose well in my defining moments. Every one of those steps involved applying truth to the various meanings I had assigned to my loss. It may sound too good to be true, but from the moment I traded God's truth for my own feelings, I have felt no pain or bitterness. Surrender can work that quickly! Now that He has cleared out my bitterness, there is room for love. I can feel that He is installing a stone of renewed love for my friend in that place which is not dependent on the restoration of our friendship.

Obedience

Obedience is a critical part of the transformation process, but a misunderstanding of the role of obedience in our spiritual journeys can actually hinder the work God is doing in us. For many years I was guilty, like some of the Galatians, of "attempting to be justified by law-keeping," but Paul teaches that this results in being "estranged from Christ" and "falling from grace."[15] I can testify to this consequence! The problem is not in our efforts to obey Him, because He tells us to keep His commandments,[16] but like so many other elements of our spiritual journey, obedience is a multi-faceted occurrence.

It is important first to recognize that we are not capable of the kind of obedience God requires. In Ezekiel 11.19, which we have looked at several times, God promises to give His people "one heart, and [to] put a new spirit within them and take the stony heart out of their flesh, and give them a heart of flesh." That's good news, but the following verse tells me why: "That they may walk in My statues and keep My judgments and do them; and they shall be My people, and I will be their God." There are two things going on here: He knows I can't obey Him without His assistance, and the expectation of His help is that I will obey Him.

He gives us those things He requires of us, confirming that even our faith is a gift from Him.[17] Paul says that though he has trust in God, it is "not that we are sufficient of ourselves to think of anything as being from ourselves, but our sufficiency is from God."[18] God Himself works in us those things that please Him, as Hebrews 13.20–21 teaches:

> Now may the God of peace who brought up our Lord Jesus from the dead, that great Shepherd of the sheep, through the blood of the everlasting covenant, make you complete in every good work to do His will, working in you what is well pleasing in His sight, through Jesus Christ, to whom be glory forever and ever. Amen.

Second, even though God promises an eternal reward for obedience, I feel sure we will recognize when we enter heaven that our inadequate obedience did not merit the magnitude of *this* reward. Paul says he has "fought the fight, finished the race, and a crown is laid up for him."[19] But look what is being done with crowns at the throne scene in Revelation 4.4–11: they're being cast down before God's throne in an apparent recognition of unworthiness. The twenty-four elders cry out, "*You* are worthy, O Lord." If even the inhabitants of heaven feel this way, it is no wonder that Scripture records the effect of the presence of God on humans as an immediate and acute awareness of our uncleanness and pathetic nature. The more we experience His presence in our lives on earth, the more we will find our sin a lot less tolerable and our obedience a lot less impressive, and on *that day,* we will know we did not earn our right to be there!

Third, our obedience is not all that remarkable to God. Isaiah, one of those men who was instantly humbled by God's presence, put it rather graphically: "All our righteousnesses are as filthy rags,"[20] Along these same lines, Jesus asked, "Does [a master] thank a servant because he did the things that were commanded him? I think not. So likewise you, when you have done all those things which you are commanded, say, 'We are unprofitable servants. We have done what was our duty to do.'"[21]

The Downside of Obedience
The downside of obedience is how our misunderstanding of it affects our temple construction. Despite apparent assistance from God, obedience is often difficult and can sometimes feel like all our own effort. It has a tendency to puff us up and make us think we're in the driver's seat, reducing our reliance on God. It can also foster and perpetuate the vending machine view of obedience that author Robert Mulholland describes: I put my quarter in (obedience), now where's my soft drink? (expected reward), which leads to resentment when I don't get what I expect.[22] This is addressed in Romans 4.4: "Now to him who works, the wages are not counted as grace but as debt."

Relying strictly on my own willpower instead of Jesus for my obedience turned out to be like walking on a thin layer of ice over a raging river. There is a place for self-control in our walk, but it can actually be counter-productive if it hinders the discovery of our abominations and the stark recognition of our need for the strength of Christ to prevail against sin. This is especially true if we naturally excel at self-control. H.A. Williams recognized these dangers when he said, "There is a sort of devilish perversity in this organizing me not to sin by means of the very thing which ensures that I shall."²³ The biggest problem with obedience through self-control is easily missed: *Self* should never be in control—Jesus should! With Him in control of our lives, our self-control becomes a fruit,²⁴ an outgrowth, not a support.

The Upside of Obedience

If even our very best efforts render us unprofitable servants, what then is the purpose of obedience? There are a lot of important reasons to obey! Though the link between obedience and results has sometimes been obvious to me, more often it has been like a key to an unknown door: I haven't always seen the connection between a certain act of obedience and a blessing I was seeking until after I obeyed—and not always then, because the blessing is a natural consequence of change within us, not a door prize for showing up.

In addition, obedience presents me to God for transformation by making me more pliable for His molding. It shows my love for Him. It helps prevent more layers of me-stones from being piled into my life, stones that must eventually be removed. Obedience teaches me the freedom found in submission. The crucifixion of myself through obedience—though painful—is only made more painful when I must experience the consequences of disobedience first. Disobedience causes pain, both to myself and to others as shown in Jabez's famous prayer, in which he says, "Keep me from evil that I might not cause pain."²⁵

So to quote Nike, just do it! Remove the uncleanness that you are able to remove from the sanctuary; God expects no less. Just don't start thinking you cleaned yourself up.

As we walk obedience's fine line, the question always to ask ourselves centers on motivation. When we read in John 14.15, "If you love me, keep my commandments," we can be guilty of working backwards and assuming our obedience reflects love. But there are many motives for obedience. It is not uncommon to obey out of coercion or a sense of duty, which are both motivated from fear of reprisal. We also might obey in order to obtain a reward. I can't say the Lord doesn't accept these motivations for obedience, since it is He who has warned us of punishment and promised us rewards. But all that He has said about fear and love teaches me that He greatly desires our motivation for obedience to be love.

Someone recently challenged me with this thought, which I pass on to you: Acting as you would act *if* you loved is not the same as loving. This differentiation of motives for obedience is truly a dividing-between-bones-and-marrow issue, which the Spirit will increasingly lead us into as we grow in Christ.

Oswald Chambers reminds us that "Sanctification makes me one with Jesus Christ, and in Him, one with God, and it is done only through the superb Atonement of Christ. Never put the effect as the cause. The *effect* in me is obedience and service and prayer, and is the *outcome* of speechless thanks and adoration for the marvelous sanctification wrought out in me *because* of the Atonement."[26] In other words, our ongoing obedience is the result of our atonement, not the way we earn it.

Trusting and obeying are not easy! They are, after all, incremental crucifixions of ourselves. But every time we choose Jesus above all else in one of these ways—whether it be in a temptation, a thought, a fear, a word or any number of other moments—we have crucified a little bit of ourselves. And in transformation, every little bit helps.

House of Prayer

When Jesus cleansed the temple, throwing out the greedy merchants in the house of God, He said, "It is written, 'My house shall be called a house of prayer,' but you have made it a 'den of thieves.'"[27] In our quest to learn everything being a temple means to us, we cannot focus solely on what is *not* to be in the temple. We can't miss that it is to be a house of *prayer.*

Virtually every event in Jesus' short life was preceded by a lengthy time spent with His Father in prayer. We are more privy to His communion with God in the Garden of Gethsemane the night before He died than in most of His other prayers. We see His sorrow and distress, as well as His need for support. He never found that support in His disciples, but He found something in His third entreaty to God that strengthened Him to face what He had to face. A powerful action took place which changed His demeanor from one of mourning to one of acceptance and determination. God apparently moved Him through the grieving process in those few hours.

If Jesus needed the Father's strength in order to endure the cross, and if we are being repeatedly led to Calvary to endure crucifixion of our worthless stones, many of which we are struggling even to identify, does it not follow that every step of the way must be bathed in prayer? I am not referring to prayers which consist mainly of asking Him to remove our problem. Although Jesus' prayers in the garden began that way, He always shifted His focus to God's desire in the situation.

I am proposing prayer which focuses more on seeking God than on asking for solutions; meditative and contemplative prayer (prayer in conjunction with Scripture), being *still* in His presence, *waiting on Him*. This narrow passageway to the altar, though difficult and time-consuming, often means less time spent on the altar. It often *is* the altar, because learning to pray unceasingly is in itself the sacrifice of attention. If we cannot navigate that tunnel, we will have greater difficulty identifying and crucifying our abominations.

We can't leave this topic without reading the "house of prayer" passage to which Jesus was referring in Matthew 21. He was quoting Isaiah 56.7:

> I will bring even Gentiles to My holy mountain, and make them joyful in My house of prayer. Their burnt offerings and their sacrifices will be accepted on My altar; for My house shall be called a house of prayer for all nations.

There is a connection between sacrifice and prayer. Prayer has a way of distilling our sacrifices down to the core. But don't miss that along with our offerings, God has promised joy. You might be able to make offerings without receiving joy, but you will not get to joy without sacrifices and prayer.

In the Word

In this chapter we have discussed many elements of the defining moment: awakening to the moment of decision, gratitude for those times we have a choice, focusing on the superior trade, trusting that God will be faithful, obeying (stepping off the platform!), and seeking the Father's guidance through this process by a lifestyle of prayer and stillness. In all of these, there is an overarching and underlying force: the absolute necessity of truth and its power to make the whole process work. We cannot hope to arrive at truth from our own perspective because our hearts are inherently deceptive[28] and we have an enemy who knows how to use that fact to his own advantage. Take it from two old-timers: Hosea said, "We have eaten the fruit of lies because we have trusted in our own way"[29] and Jeremiah knew that "it is not in man to direct his own steps."[30] We must consult God's written truth along with His Spirit's guidance if we are to know the truth that will set us free. We must know God, and we must know His Word if we hope to know what to do when presented with the defining moments in our lives.

The Stubbornness of Stone

Richard Wilbur's poem *Two Voices in the Meadow*[31] describes the surrender of a milkweed, whose ruptured pod initiates the exchange of a root-bound existence for a life of air-borne influence and freedom. It is elevated to higher identity and posterity simply by agreeing to be shattered into a new form.

This is contrasted with the heavy inertia of stone, content to lie in earthy oblivion, unaffected by the same wind that frees the milkweed. The stone's perspective is that accepting or initiating change feels like the world is tipping precariously on its axis—or as Wilbur put it, "The sill of heaven founders." It feels its job is to hold things together, to prevent insecurity and the sense of precariousness surrender produces by protecting the status quo, by becoming a squatter in whatever spot it finds itself. If that describes you, remember that you serve a Savior who loved to shake things up!

A Milkweed

Anonymous as cherubs
Over the crib of God,
White seeds are floating
Out of my burst pod.
What power had I
Before I learned to yield?
Shatter me, great wind:
I shall possess the field.

A Stone

As casual as cow-dung
Under the crib of God,
I lie where chance would have me,
Up to the ears in sod.
Why should I move? To move
Befits a light desire.
The sill of heaven would founder,
Did such as I aspire.

Open Your Heart

Enjoying the House

When love beckons to you, follow him
Though his ways are hard and steep.

And when his wings enfold you, yield to him,
Though the sword hidden among his pinions may wound you.

And when he speaks to you believe in him,
Though his voice may shatter your dreams as the north wind lays
waste the garden

For even as love crowns you so shall he crucify you.
Even as he is for your growth so he is for your pruning.

Even as he ascends to your heights and caresses your tenderest
branches that quiver in the sun,
So shall he descend to your roots and shake them in
their clinging to the earth.

Kahlil Gibran, *The Prophet*

9

The Total Perspective Vortex
You Are Here

*"Someday, after mastering the winds, the waves, the tides and gravity,
we shall harness for God the energies of love, and then, for a second time
in the history of the world, man will have discovered fire."*
Pierre Teilhard de Chardin

A young minister's beloved wife and infant daughter die. The man who declares God to others must now wrestle with that same God. He finds that explaining away suffering is a lot harder to do when it is his suffering. He spends the next 50 years struggling to reconcile his great sorrow and loneliness with what he has believed about God. Resigning himself to a life of solitude, yet choosing to hold on to God, he finds love half a century later with a much younger woman who bears him a son. His life begins again, but he is given less than a decade of happiness before his 80-something year-old heart shows imminent signs of wearing out.

It is from this vantage that John Ames, the dying minister in Marilynne Robinson's Pulitzer-Prize winning novel *Gilead*, attempts to gather up his accumulated musings and experiences into some kind of useful package for the son he will not see grow to adulthood. Like a sieve, the effort to capture an entire lifespan all at once distills that which is valuable from that which is meaningless. His sadness, confusion and shortcomings must be weighed in the final accounting, but what rises to the surface is a legacy full of hope and peace, described in part this way:

> There are two occasions when the sacred beauty of Creation becomes dazzlingly apparent, and they occur together. One is when we feel our *moral insufficiency* to the world, and the other is when we feel the world's *mortal insufficiency* to us. Augustine says the Lord loves each of us as an only child and that has to be true. 'He will wipe the tears from all faces.' It takes nothing from the loveliness of the verse to say that is exactly what will be required.[1]

The Insufficiency of it All

There is no doubt that the history of our world has been tumultuous and that its current plight remains unsolvable. Despite social evolution and massive progressive technologies wherein a kid with an Internet connection can communicate with someone on the other side of the globe, mankind has failed to solve the ancient quandaries of the human condition. We may hear about an earthquake in China within minutes of its occurrence, yet we are largely unable to solve the crisis. And our technology certainly does nothing to prevent the earthquake in the first place.

In addition to this impotence, there is the hitch that human progress ultimately creates new dilemmas and disasters, though we may not recognize them for generations. Then there are the deliberate atrocities men and women perpetrate on society—war, genocide, racism, abortion and more. There is also the reality that even our substantial efforts for good—to end poverty, for example—do not cure the world's problems. Poverty persists, just as Jesus said it would. "The poor you have with you always"[2] stands as a testimony to the fact *we are morally insufficient for the world*. If we cannot fix ourselves, the only part of our existence over which we have any real control, how can we hope to cure the whole thing? Jesus said that if one blind person tries to lead another blind person, they will both fall in the ditch.[3] We're all broken, and a broken thing cannot mend itself or anything else.

It is also true that the *world is mortally insufficient to us*. Despite its often breathtaking beauty, vast supplies, and promise of potential joy, it is a place of pain and death. The result of all these things we cannot fix is that it is difficult to feel comfortable for more than a few moments; struggles and tears are unavoidable, times of deep joy and peace are hard-won and fleeting. King Solomon testified that all the resources available to him—and he had access to them all!—were not sufficient to answer the longings of the human heart. Each generation's continued efforts to find satisfaction, relief and long-term happiness with those same visible resources create an endless loop, both in societies and in our mortal bodies. We are dying and nothing this world has to offer can change that. Even if we could make significant headway in fixing the world, it could not change our mortal destiny.

Dazzled By Creation

Despite the existence of death and pain, sometimes life takes our breath away with its unexpected joys. Occasionally we transcend a boundary to discover something for which we have exhaustively searched but could not find. Like a snake shedding its skin, we experience a season of discomfort that opens up to a fresh awareness that had been blocked by the very skin we were in. These little miracles feed our growing suspicion that our perspectives are pitifully small.

But John Ames says we can see the sacred beauty of our existence with dazzling clarity in another moment, a moment that does not seem miraculous: it is when we see both extremes of insufficiency at the same time. Independently of each other, they create hopelessness. Together, they make us weep, but they create a contrast for the tears: the promise that those tears will be wiped away.[4]

Not dried up. Not forgotten. Wiped away. The comforting Creator—who does not invalidate pain but heals it—will not simply distract us from our grief with the flashiness of heaven. I don't imagine our tears being wiped away the way we delete files from the hard drives of our computers, sending them into cyberspace—whatever that is. There is something infinitely more personal happening with our tears. I like to imagine His hand cupping the side of my face and His gigantic thumb sweeping my tears away, while He acknowledges my pain and tells me it's alright now.

He is masterful at healing the pain that produced those tears, but though I may forget that pain, He does not. David says that God has a bottle where He puts our tears.[5] Could it be that He keeps track of our sorrows, that they have some kind of inherent worth which we do not see? It appears to me that the thumb that sweeps my tears away does not cast them aside, but absorbs them into His being, transforming them somehow into my glory.

During the darkest season of my life, I found a great deal of comfort in the book of Hebrews, which explores these themes, contrasting them to the suffering of Jesus. Twice we are told to consider Him when we search for answers to our suffering.[6] Like those lilies He told us to consider, I found that important messages in His suffering are interminably intertwined with my sorrows.

To begin with, I was made for glory and honor.[7] Once sin entered the world, it became necessary that I work to see past my pain to that original intent. When I see that the suffering of Jesus crowned *Him* with glory and honor,[8] I realize that *my* suffering is the raw material for my glory.

The King James Version of the Bible calls Jesus the "captain of our salvation;" the newer ones describe Him as the "author of our salvation." These words encompass the concepts of responsibility, leadership and source. I especially like the image of Jesus as captain. It reinforces the journey aspect of our suffering. In the same way that the captain of a ship is on board that ship throughout the voyage, Jesus participates in our passage through life. Not only did He become the way to reach God,[9] He took that same way Himself—which included suffering. In His efforts to bring "many sons to glory, it was fitting...*that He be made* perfect through suffering."[10] The purpose was to destroy Satan and to release me from my life sentence of bondage, and to become a High Priest who is able pour out mercy on His people.[11]

Immediately following that revelation is a "therefore" that explains the response we should have to this knowledge. Among that depiction, I was surprised by references to the building of a house: that "He who built the house has more honor than the house. For every house is built by someone, but He who built all things is God. Moses was faithful in His house as a servant, but Christ is a Son over God's house, whose house *we are* if we hold fast the confidence and the rejoicing of the hope firm to the end." [12] I do not believe the end to be merely the end of our lives, but the end of every season of suffering, for though "weeping endures for the night, joy comes in the morning." [13]

Hebrews 12.1–3 tells us to look "to Jesus, the author and finisher of our faith, who for the joy that was set before Him endured the cross." The good news is that *we are that joy.* In return, as we "consider His endurance" when we are weary and discouraged, He is the joy that becomes our strength.[14] When I held fast to Him in my suffering, I came to understand the joy that we are to each other.

In the face of the realities of human and terrestrial insufficiency I have been immensely comforted by that which *is* sufficient: "My grace is sufficient for you, for My strength is made perfect in weakness." [15] And it is this perspective which has changed my life.

Perspectives

The word *perspective* denotes an angle of vision, with superior perspectives emphasizing the panoramic lens. A myopic examination focuses on a single element, one piece of the puzzle, while the panoramic view includes what the picture on the box looks like. Both views are necessary and valid. You cannot consider the message of lilies without studying them minutely, but you cannot learn all there is to learn simply from researching lilies apart from their ecological systems, and that system's inclusion in greater systems. In those moments when we get a glimpse of a bigger perspective, Henri Nouwen dares us to "choose to claim them as God's way of tapping us on our shoulders and showing us the deepest truth of our existence."

Ideally, life is a series of broadening perspectives, yet without a loving God, a clear realization of our place in the universe would be a very scary thing. Author Douglas Adams recognized and included this concept in his book *The Restaurant at the End of the Universe*, the second installment of his satirical descriptions of the cosmos.[16] In this story, the character Trin Tragula creates the Total Perspective Vortex, a device designed to give his wife a perspective of the infinite nature of the universe. No one could survive the Total Perspective Vortex because the conscious mind could not tolerate its own lack of significance in proportion to infinity, but neither Trin nor his wife knew that.

> "Have some sense of proportion!" she would say, sometimes as often as thirty-eight times in a single day.
>
> And so he built the Total Perspective Vortex, just to show her. Into one end he plugged the whole of reality as extrapolated from a piece of fairy cake, and into the other end he plugged his wife: so that when he turned it on she saw in one instant the whole infinity of creation and herself in relation to it.
>
> To Trin Tragula's horror, the shock completely annihilated her brain; but to his satisfaction he realized that he had proved conclusively that if life is going to exist in a Universe of this size, then the one thing it cannot have is a sense of proportion.[17]

Though Adams brilliantly and humorously takes on the unanswerable questions of the universe, his perspective as an atheist seeps into his Total Perspective Vortex. It reminds me of the methods even believers employ in order to cope with our little lives when we don't recognize God as consistently benevolent and good. Our hopelessness, fear and doubt require that we build very small, manageable worlds in which to exist, and even smaller, more manageable boxes to put God in.

In Trin's Total Perspective Vortex, what one sees is "a momentary glimpse of the entire unimaginable infinity of creation, and somewhere in it a tiny little marker, a microscopic dot on a microscopic dot, which says 'You Are Here.'" I am convinced that if we could see into God's Total Perspective Vortex, what we would see is a realm of love.

The Greatest Thing

Love, as I have mangled it, is itself a topic that can overwhelm. I have not been very good at the giving of love for much of my life, and even worse at receiving it. Yet I have discovered the truth in the poet Rumi's observation: "Your task is not to seek for love, but merely to seek and find all the barriers within yourself that you have built against it." All my efforts to love from my own strength were well-intentioned, but fell far short of pleasing anybody.

When I began to understand how God is building me into a holy temple and to submit to the removal of pieces of myself, I discovered an incredible energy—it felt like happiness, peace, unlimited vision, creativity, magnanimity, and complete security— all at the same time. All I could do was wonder if this was the gift of Romans 5.5, which says, "The love of God has been poured out in our hearts." This overwhelming force floods me from within every time I crucify something that opposes God or truth or love. For me, that is anything I am clinging to or leaning on other than Him. It is not so much a reward as the natural consequence of removing barriers. Let me remind you again, those barriers are chunks of *me*.

Before I experienced this in such an overwhelming way, I got glimpses of it in my suffering. The early Celtic Christians had a name for those times or places when the boundary between the sacred and the everyday feels "thin," when God's presence is more strongly felt. They called them "thin places." When I began to recognize that I existed within a realm of love, all of life—and *especially my struggles*[18]—became thin places. My most intimate moments with God have occurred during times of pain. This was not because He is more accessible during those times, but because *I am*. These experiences have taught me that no matter where the "You Are Here" marker pointed in God's Total Perspective Vortex—whether it was to times of suffering, struggle, silence or smooth sailing—it was all taking place within a sphere of His love for me.

At the heart of this sphere of love is the cross of Christ. This moment in time, this supreme marker of God's love for us, is where the sacred beauty of Creation truly is centered, for "God demonstrated His own love toward us, in that while we were still sinners, Christ died for us."[19] Although His suffering does help us to comprehend our own suffering, something so much more powerful is accomplished at the cross than simply being able to relate.

At the cross, my insufficiency to the *world* is solved by the nails He took for me; no other path exists to take care of the problem in the world that is me. At the cross, the world's insufficiency to *me* is addressed by the solution to death—His resurrection. The only path that leads to my resurrection is this: if I participate in the fellowship of His suffering, I will also share in the power of His resurrection![20] The removal of me-stones and the replacement with Christ-stones *is* the suffering that puts me as close to the cross as I can be.

The Prerogative of an Author

We began our journey together comparing the elements of story which are found in literature to the details of our lives. The common element all stories share is an author who has complete freedom to write his story any way he chooses. Considering our topic, Jesus as the author or *writer* of our salvation is a logical application. The absurdity of readers (or characters) dictating that storyline is captured with chilling horror in Stephen King's *Misery*,[21] the story of a novelist who is injured in a car accident and trapped in a snowstorm shortly after finishing the final book in a popular series that has made him famous. A psychotic nurse named Annie Wilkes who believes herself to be his number one fan rescues him and takes care of him through the storm. When she discovers that he has killed off the main character, Misery, in order to move into a different type of writing, she breaks his ankles to keep him from escaping, while trying to force him to write another storyline that keeps Misery alive.

At one time or another, we all feel like Annie Wilkes about the story of our lives, wanting it to be rewritten to fit our personal vision or trying to forcibly write ourselves. Or we may feel that God is like Annie Wilkes, hobbling us to keep us from escaping the storyline He is writing for us. The perspective we need to have is that the purposes of the author are the only truth we have to work with. Until we're big enough to hold God's pen, the story we would write would not have the best conclusion possible, for we would settle for something far less wonderful than the adventure and victorious ending in store for us. With our finite perspective, I'm sure we would—like Annie Wilkes— keep *misery* alive.

Perspectives have consequences. If we view God's authorship of our lives as a concept that rationalizes intentional pain in favor of the vaguely theoretical purpose of building us into a temple that is Christ—and that this is for *His* sake, not ours—we will see God only as a cruel manipulator, an author unattached to his characters, or a bin-tipping teenager torturing a turtle. And this perspective will block the realization of love.

I suppose if a little kid had the ability to think this way, that is how she would feel about being taken to the emergency room for stitches or surgery. When I was little and sick and didn't understand how the body works, it made no sense that causing more pain with needles and knives would make me feel better. Yet, we adults know this is true, and we allow the pain inflicted upon our children when they are sick because we love them.

Do you remember when we read in Matthew 20 that Jesus was hailed as king and that He first proceeded in Matthew 21 to cleanse the temple and *then* set about His business of healing the sick? There is sickness and pain in each stone of me. The metaphor of the deconstruction of the temple that followed is like the surgery that a doctor must perform. The healing process hurts as it makes contact with our disease. What we feel is the pain of being rebuilt from a pile of rocks to a glorious temple. God's goal is not to *cause* pain nor to simply *banish* pain, but to restore complete health, freedom and life as we have never known it.

Nothing Can Separate Us From His Love

Every generation has pondered the question of whether love and suffering are mutually exclusive. The Author of love chose Paul to address that question in Romans 8, which is so important to this discussion that we must examine His thoughts on the subject.

Paul says, "If we suffer with Christ, we will be glorified with Him." [22] We have seen in the temple how suffering builds us to a point of being able to experience the glory of the Son of Man. Somehow, the suffering we endure now is so small compared to the glory to be revealed in us that Paul says it is not even worth comparing. [23] Faith requires that we trust in this unrealized perspective. That feat is easier when I remember that the magnitude of all pain is continually diminishing once it is over. All I have to do is recall any physical injury to determine this truth. Jesus made that exact point in John 16.21–22:

> A woman, when she is in labor, has sorrow because her hour has come; but as soon as she has given birth to the child, she no longer remembers the anguish, for joy that a human being has been born into the world. Therefore you now have sorrow; but I will see you again and your heart will rejoice, and your joy no one will take from you.

Birth is on Paul's mind too, who says our suffering is part of a bigger picture. "All creation suffers, groaning as it labors toward its redemption in eternity." [24] It is somewhat mind-numbing to imagine that our entire world, our entire existence, is in a birth process! No pregnant woman expects to bring forth the wonderful miracle of a baby without enduring the trials of pregnancy: morning sickness, cravings, stretch marks, heartburn, swelling, carrying a heavy weight, contractions (formerly called *labor pains)* and delivery. Paul's metaphor not only helps me put the insufficiencies of the world into perspective, but it sets me to wondering what the outcome of such a huge labor and delivery process as the one we are experiencing will be! It also reminds me once again that the effects of resistance to this birth process must be similar to my resistance in childbirth, which required my doctor to tell me that if I transferred the energy I was investing in yelling to pushing, we would be done a lot sooner.

It is here, in the context of suffering, that we find the promise we have been discussing in depth: "All things work together for good to those who love God, to those who are called according to His purpose." [25] That purpose, that *good*, is our being "conformed to the image of His dear Son." [26] This used to sound rather dubious to me. It was so far away from reality as to have little meaning to me. Was the good only to be realized if I made it to heaven? Perhaps it was a thing that blessed God and His purposes in the present somehow, but was there good to be found there for me in this life?

I have stumbled onto the realization that His image in us reveals all the things we have been seeking! In becoming the image of Jesus, we find a wellspring of love, joy, peace, hope, and comfort. Paul's references in his second letter to Timothy of the "promises of life," [27] "His purpose and grace" [28] and "faith and love" which are found "in Christ," [29] are given full expression in us when He is in us. God comes near to us in the most intimate way possible.

Just as God's love doesn't preclude suffering for us, suffering doesn't preclude His love for us. Paul speaks in the same way that any who have glimpsed the dimensions of love do: trying to show its limitlessness, its omnipresence, its power and its value above all we might endure:

> Can anything ever separate us from Christ's love? Does it mean he no longer loves us if we have trouble or calamity, or are persecuted, or are hungry or cold or in danger or threatened with death? (Even the Scriptures say, "For your sake we are killed every day; we are being slaughtered like sheep.") No, despite all these things, overwhelming victory is ours through Christ, who loved us. And I am convinced that nothing can ever separate us from his love. Death can't, and life can't. The angels can't, and the demons can't. Our fears for today, our worries about tomorrow, and even the powers of hell can't keep God's love away. Whether we are high above the sky or in the deepest ocean, nothing in all creation will ever be able to separate us from the love of God that is revealed in Christ Jesus our Lord. [30]

The few glimpses I've been granted of the permeation of love throughout everything leave me stuttering, stammering and ultimately speechless, as a true perspective of anything pertaining to God tends to do (if it doesn't fry your brain!). Love is not simply a feeling or an act of our will, but energy and power. If God is love, then love in any form is God at work. The power of love is the power of God and we are filled with it to overflowing. Think about verse 18 again: our sufferings are nothing compared to the glory "which shall be revealed *in* us." Revealed *in* us, not *to* us. This is that love that "has been poured out in our hearts." [31]

The ultimate epiphany is seeing that love emerge from under the layers of rubble He has been removing. When I have had an infection cured, a pile of debris in my heart swept out, or the pain of a loss healed by His touch, what I always find underneath is love, an expansive love that completely takes me by surprise. I don't just feel better, I feel loved and I love everyone—not just my friends and family, but all of humanity! I feel love for the beauty and wisdom of the divine, which, to my surprise, encompasses even my suffering. The energy of God's love that infuses our world has shimmered into my consciousness a few times. It is glorious! I can most accurately describe it as the experience of falling in love, only with eyes and heart wide open.

Gravity Works

In addition, I find that things I once worked hard to do become automatic responses, like obedience to gravity. Obedience to natural laws is… well, natural. You don't have to work at it. If you step off a building, you will fall with no effort. When I am operating within the experience of God's love, gratitude no longer becomes an act of my will, but an overflowing emotion. I am astonished to realize that "he who loves God must love his brother also" [32] is not so much a command to follow, but one of those natural laws. It is impossible to truly see the love of God and not have two responses: to fall in love with Him in return, and to fall into love for my brother.

Love is the overarching feature of our transformations, but there are several considerations of that love which I have had to sort out. The first is that we like to believe that if something doesn't feel good, it isn't good. If my modern human definition of love is the lens through which I interpret the events of my life, I will fail to see God's love at work in my life. But if I interpret my experiences through the lens of absolute trust in His declaration of love, whether it matches my definition of love or not, I get a completely different outcome, one which bears good fruit, not resentment, confusion and bitterness.

Second, when Paul says that "all things work together for good *for those who love the Lord,* to those who are called according to His purpose," I am forced to ponder how my love for Him impacts this process. Anyone who has responded to His call has some level of love for God, due to the natural laws at work around Him. Looking back, my love for Him was so pitifully small as to be little more than opening my hand to receive a trillion dollars, yet there is no doubt that He has brought me into the natural law of reclamation and restoration promised in this passage. Jesus is able to work with even a mustard seed's amount of faith;[33] He does not begin or continue His work in our lives on anything from us but the tiniest show of cooperation. After all, He must teach us how to love. At no point does He expect us to be experts at it apart from Him.

Third, John said, "We love Him because He first loved us." Our love is response. *His* love is the basis of all healing, as we see in the resurrection of dead Lazarus. Mary and Martha sent word to Jesus saying, "Lord, he whom *you love* is sick."[34]

Awake and Unafraid

Fear is one of our biggest barriers to experiencing God's love. If "perfect love casts out fear,"[35] then fear is evidence that the flow of His perfect love has been stifled. And though our efforts to love Him and experience His love will never be perfect, it is through these efforts that we endure the journey of being built by Him. Leo Tolstoy said, "All, everything I understand, I understand because I love." Somehow, when we are able to receive and reciprocate His love, we understand a little bit better.

The process I have been describing can be disheartening and

scary for those who haven't been through a bout or two of trans-formation and seen Jesus up-close and personal. The more I see Him, the closer I come to embracing this journey as an adventure. I no longer want to enter this venture of faith like I'm walking the plank to my doom. This is what Kierkegaard calls "the greatest falsehood": that "my immense resignation would be a substitute for faith." [36] It's easy to be confused about that.

Resignation is acceptance, but with a twist. It is the acceptance of despair, [37] rather than an embracing of hope. And when we ac-cept despair, that is what we will have. Resentment soon follows, and we are left wondering why God has failed us. There was a time I thought I had faith, but when real faith began to show up, invited in by my decision to stop resisting my life, I could clearly see that earlier I had been simply resigning myself to an inferior fate, not joyfully accepting that my trials existed within God's highest plan for my life. Resignation was a pale substitute for the living color found in real faith, even in its mustard seed phase.

Instead of resignation, consider the concept of exuberantly welcoming God's work in you. In 2 Corinthians 1.18–20 we find that kind of exuberance attributed to Christ:

> But as God is faithful, our word to you was not Yes and No. For the Son of God, Jesus Christ, who was preached among you by us…was not Yes and No, but in Him was Yes. For all the prom-ises of God in Him are Yes, and in Him Amen, to the glory of God through us.

Through my own strength, I have lived out my journey as *Perhaps* and *No*, sometimes tentatively cooperating and participating, oth-er times crawling under the covers and yelling "NO MORE!" but Jesus fulfills all of God's promises with a "Yes" and an "Amen!" Through His strength, I am becoming a person who throws wide my arms and says "Yes" and "Amen" to the sanctification of my sanctuary, and "Yes" to the adventure God has designed for me. That adventure is not simply the life I see, but what that life looks like from above His wings.

What Victory Looks Like

I used to believe that God-pleasing faith and love must look like a sprint across the finish line, arms raised in victory. That was before I took a few laps around the track, falling, and falling behind. I felt a magnetic spark of recognition and hope for what my finish might look like when I heard about Derek Redmond, the Olympic runner from England who was engaged in what he knew would be his last hope for the Olympics—the 1992 Summer Olympics in Barcelona, Spain. His hamstring tore when he was 175 meters from the finish line in the semi-finals.

Against unspeakable pain, he got up, shrugged away the men with the stretcher, and began limping toward the finish line, determined to finish. His father, who was his coach, emerged from the stands, pushed through security, crossed onto the track, and lifted his son's arm around his shoulder, helping him hobble the last leg of the race. He released Derek to cross over the finish line alone. Derek didn't come close to winning, but the tears and roar of the crowd declared Derek Redmond a hero. A video of this event is available online. [38] I urge you to see this compelling picture of what finishing looks like, and also what it means to finish on the strength of the Father. (Bring tissues. This story ranks 77th in the top 100 televised tearjerkers. [39])

The fact is, if victory can look like this at the finish line, in the middle I might look broken and bleeding, as Jesus was in his final hours. I probably will be at times weak and inadequate, as Peter was in the courtyard. I'm positive that occasionally I'll only be advancing because I'm being carried, as the man who was let down on a cot through the roof so Jesus could heal him. The state of being bent and bruised is not a disappointment to God, as I earlier believed. It is the reality of the human condition, both for believers and unbelievers at various points in our journey.

In his song "Hallelujah," Leonard Cohen declares that "Love is not a victory march, it's a cold and it's a broken hallelujah." [40] Though I don't espouse the idea that all things of God must be painful, neither can I cling to the idea that love should not be difficult. If God's demonstrated love to me included His Son dying on a cross, then *true* love will not always appear triumphant this side of heaven. Love is sometimes a hoarsely whispered "praise *Him*" when all around me is falling apart. That "praise *Him*" maintains the connection to love that has provided the courage and the reason to persevere in my 29-year old marriage. I have seen that sooner or later, in one way or another, love will be victorious because "love never fails." [41] It will eventually produce something. Then we will see, as Jacob did, that "Surely the presence of the Lord was even in this dark place."

Victory in the Struggle

At the beginning of our time together, I asked you to be willing to struggle. There's no getting around that. We *will* struggle. I mentioned in chapter 7 the physical struggle Jacob had with God, for which he was rewarded. It happened on his way to El Bethel. He had fearfully prayed for a welcome reception at his reunion with his brother Esau. That night, he had the odd experience of wrestling with an angel until daybreak. The angel tried to end the contest but Jacob would not let Him go until He gave him a blessing. The blessing was a new name. Because he had "struggled with God and man, and prevailed," his name was changed from Jacob *(Deceiver)* to Israel *(Prince with God)*. [42]

After that, Jacob asked the angel's name but was not given an answer. Instead, he received another blessing. The receipt of a blessing will always be more valuable than the satisfying of our curiosity. As commentator Matthew Henry says, "The tree of life is better than the tree of knowledge." And yet Jacob's blessing appears to have included the certain knowledge that he had been wrestling with God and that the blessing was due to God's mercy, not his own strength because he says, "I have seen God face to face, and my life is preserved." [43] The point for us is that the development of our faith is essentially a struggle against God. Like Jacob, we must refuse to let go of Him until we start to receive His promised blessings. (And then we won't want to let go!)

I was very excited to see that Revelation 2.17 promises to those who overcome, "I will give him a white stone, and on the stone a new name [is] written which no one knows except him who receives it." I have often thought it was a shame that the deceased have to miss all the wonderful things people say about them at their funerals, but how infinitely better to be met in heaven by Jesus presenting us with the final stone for our temple, engraved with our new name, saying, "Here's what I thought about you!"

God sheds a little more light on the relationship between victory and struggle by putting Jacob's transformation in terms of day and night. Verse 31 tells us what immediately followed his encounter with the angel. "Just as he crossed over Penuel, the sun rose on him." Author Nathan Ward points out in his commentary on Genesis, *The Growth of the Seed,* that not only is a "new day of light dawning for Jacob," but,

> [His] time away from Canaan [can also be seen] as a period of darkness. The sun set on him as he departed the Promised Land (28.11), having stolen the blessing that God intended to give him. Here, as he returns, the sun rises... just as he returns to the Promised Land.[44]

Never abandoned during the trials of those dark years, Jacob fulfilled a departure and return that constituted the exact length of a divinely-appointed night.

William Blake used an interesting phrase in his poem "The Little Black Boy."[45] He said "And we are put on earth a little space. ...That we may learn to bear the beams of love." He expresses in this way both our life's purpose and its difficulty: to love and be loved by God

If we are going to struggle, then let's, as parents like to say, choose our battles. When I became willing to struggle with the suffering that accompanies learning the spiritual significance of everything in my life, discovering my true self, letting that person go bit by bit, and leaning on God with all my weight, I did so because it was the only choice that gave meaning to the path we are all on.

If we struggle with *these* things, one day we will look up from our circular wanderings and see that something was built from nothing, that good was worked from our bad. The sun will rise on a temple that has been being built in the dark, surprising us with what has been accomplished. We will find a temple with all the attributes of that physical temple we discussed in chapter two: power, sanctuary, strength and the presence of Jesus. It is a house built *of* love, *by* love, and *for* love.

If we haven't struggled with *these* things, all we've done is gone in circles.

Epilogue

The Face of the Father

"Philip said to Him, 'Lord, show us the Father, and it is sufficient for us.'"
John 14.8

Whether or not you have grasped all that I hoped to pass on to you in this book, years from now you will have begun to see this process for yourself. You will have survived many transformation periods and actually triumphed over some of them. You will have recognized the tangled concepts of love and suffering as you have seen your own growth blossom from those rich soils. As you have mastered the art of self-crucifixion, you will be developing into a noticeably well-built temple as Jesus becomes more and more a part of your basic make-up. You will have started to look like Job.

Job was very successful—"the greatest man in the East"—and the father of ten children. He regularly prayed and offered sacrifices not only for his own sins, but for his children's. Spiritually, he was "blameless, upright, feared God, and shunned evil." This is the ultimate goal for which many Christians strive, right? To master the discipline of praying consistently. To be blameless. To have a good reputation. By our standards, Job had arrived.

Then God allowed Satan to initiate chaos and pain into Job's life. Job's almost superhuman responses to unbelievable horror show the kind of temple he had become. He praised God even though he had lost everything. He refused to curse God even though his body was wracked with pain. If you only read the first two chapters of the narrative, it is difficult not to be dismayed by what God seems to be doing, yet this is just the prologue, the establishment of the setting and introduction of the characters. When considered in the context of holy temple building, the dialogue between Job and his friends in chapters 4–37, and between God and Job in chapters 38–42, contains the real story of Job.

Journey to the Heart of God

Job teaches us that when we think we have learned all we can learn, God is not done with us yet. In the building process, Job had become a complex wonder of a temple, far advanced in its construction, with walls of deep faith and trust dotted throughout with a few stones of doubt and confusion. Though he was blameless and trusted God, his conversation with his friends and with God exposed some stones that needed replacing—and these, if you remember from chapter 6, are the rendezvous points with God. Job is evidence to me that as we travel deeper and deeper into the heart of God, He is doing the same in us, bringing us to spiritual heights we cannot even imagine.

To get there, Job experienced many of the elements of deconstruction we saw in Matthew 24: The loss of all his children and possessions was the initial *earthquake* that rocked his world.[1] He experienced *pestilence* as he was struck with painful boils and left to scrape himself with broken pottery while he sat in ashes,[2] and *betrayal* when his wife encouraged him to curse God.[3] He triumphed in these defining moments, but that was just the *beginning of sorrows.*

In his despair, Job revealed stones of *fear* and *anxiety.*[4] Remember Kierkegaard's idea that anxiety and freedom are linked? Anxiety is evidence of impending change, that something else is about to be discovered. The trial was not simply a test to see if he would renounce God, but the initiation of a deeper transformation episode than he had ever experienced. He was nearing a discovery and he sensed it was going to get worse before it got better.

In chapters 4 to 37, Job and his friends had an increasingly heated dialogue that might be construed metaphorically as *war.* Their pushback was experienced by Job as scorn,[5] torment,[6] and "miserable comfort"[7]—might we call it *persecution* and *betrayal*? Job's defenses indicated that he was experiencing both physical and spiritual *famine*, and *confusion*. He searched through his heart to find a flaw, but could not find one, repeatedly *running back to his confidence* in his righteousness. Though Job had friends to support him, he was unable to experience that support because this was a time when he needed to hear only God. What that felt like to him was *loneliness*. He experienced a prolonged period of *waiting* on God

Elihu's speech in chapters 32–36 reveals the problem with Job and his friends' understanding about God, which are their veiled stones. They admitted to God's power and sovereignty, but in their resignation (acceptance of despair) they did not see God's compassion, goodness and fairness. Elihu understood that Job's affliction was not punishment for sin, but for purification, for transformation, and that the only appropriate answer was to wait for God to "teach [us] what we do not see."[8] He made it profoundly simple: do not choose iniquity over affliction.[9] You're going to struggle… struggle where there is hope. Struggling with God *in our affliction* results in blessing. Adding sin into the mix is only going to compound the struggle.

Unlike his older friends, Job refused to resort to resignation, revealing his advanced readiness for God to go deeper. He did not even know that this willing courage was a part of his makeup, but God did. To God, Job's blamelessness meant he was equipped to be stretched for greater joy and disclosure than he had ever experienced.

Seeing God

Job saw his stone in the same moment he saw God. When God began to speak, He did not justify His actions or address Job's righteousness or sin; He said, in essence, "Here's who I AM, who do you think *you* are?" This will always be the crux of the matter. When we see God—*really see Him*—words are no longer necessary. We simultaneously see ourselves and the truth cannot be denied: "I am vile. I will shut my mouth."[10] Job's ultimate defining moment showed that he was ready to surrender the stone that presumed to exalt itself as more right than God: "I have uttered what I did not understand, things too wonderful for me, which I did not know… I have heard of you by the hearing of the ear, but now my eye sees You. Therefore I abhor myself and repent in dust and ashes." [11]

Joseph Campbell powerfully sums up this scene:

> There is no word of explanation, no mention of the dubious wager with Satan described in chapter one… only a thunder-and-lightning demonstration of the fact of facts, namely that man cannot measure the will of God, which derives from a center beyond the range of human categories. Categories, indeed, are totally shattered by the Almighty of the Book of Job, and remain shattered to the last. Nevertheless, to Job himself the revelation appears to have made soul-satisfying sense. He was a hero who, by his courage in the fiery furnace… had proven himself capable of facing a greater revelation than the one that satisfied his friends. We cannot interpret his words in the last chapter as those of a man merely intimidated. They are the words of one who has seen something surpassing anything that has been said by way of justification. …For the son who has grown really to know the father, the agonies of the ordeal are readily borne; the world is no longer a vale of tears but a bliss-yielding, perpetual manifestation of the Presence. [12]

Restitution, Restoration and Reclamation

As the seasons attest, the natural law of loss and death is restoration and rebirth. While God was primarily concerned with restoration in Job's soul, He did not neglect his physical life:

> And the Lord restored Job's losses when he prayed for his friends. Indeed the Lord gave Job twice as much as he had before. Then all his brothers, all his sisters, and all those who had been his acquaintances before, came to him and ate food with him in his house; and they consoled him and comforted him for all the adversity that the Lord had brought upon him. Each one gave him a piece of silver and each a ring of gold. Now the Lord blessed the latter days of Job more than his beginning; for he had fourteen thousand sheep, six thousand camels, one thousand yoke of oxen, and one thousand female donkeys. He also had seven sons

and three daughters…in all the land were found no women so beautiful as the daughters of Job; and their father gave them an inheritance among their brothers. After this Job lived one hundred and forty years, and saw his children and grandchildren for four generations. So Job died, old and full of days. [13]

We all know some things can never be replaced. The ten new children Job had did not replace the ten he lost. But the phrase "full of days" means Job lived out his life fully and happily. His heart was restored in a way that mere replacement of loss could never do. His heart was full of God.

Corrie Ten Boom said, "You may never know that Jesus is all you need, until Jesus is all you have." That we cannot see how Job recovered only indicates that we have not yet traveled to the end of the path he traveled. The terror of his story is that our souls might be destined to a similar emotional disemboweling at the hand of an arbitrarily unmerciful God. Yet Job's transcendence above the apparent ruthlessness of the Lord is accomplished by a glimpse of the source of his terror. As Campbell says, "He sees the face of the father, understands—and the two are atoned." [14]

On Our Knees
Experiencing the fullness of God in a lasting and meaningful way is the reward for a seasoned and intimate relationship with Him. And that takes time. God's interaction with Job shows me that He will never be through with me. No matter how good I start to look, no matter how blameless I become, there will always be room for God to go deeper. I will never be through being transformed until I am in heaven!

Author Harold Brodkey said, "I distrust summaries, any kind of gliding through time, any too great a claim that one is in control of what one recounts; I think someone who claims to understand but is obviously calm, someone who claims to write with emotion recollected in tranquility, is a fool and a liar. To understand is to tremble. To recollect is to re-enter and be riven. …I admire the authority of being on one's knees in front of the event." [15]

I especially second the notion that any authority over our stories emerges from trembling and from "being on one's knees in front of the event." It is a perpetual requirement for the journey: humility, a sense of awe, a willingness to keep admitting you only have specks of wisdom, glimpses of triumph, a fragile trust, a propensity for fear and a tendency to try to run the show.

My prayer is that over time when you feel desolate, you will remember the temple. When you feel hammered, sawn, sanded and planed, you will think of the tabernacle. When you feel your world shaking all to bits, thoughts of the sanctuary will remind you that the House of Love the Lord is building of you—the temple made of Jesus, to make room for Jesus—cannot be shaken.

Everything else has to go.

Notes

Open Your Eyes: Seeing the House Plans
Chapter One – Making Sense out of Change
[1] Carl Jung, Editor Joseph Campbell, *The Portable Jung* (England: Penguin Books, LTD., 1977) 523.
[2] Brennan Manning, *The Ragamuffin Gospel* (United States: Multnomah Publishers, 1990, 2000) 15.
[3] Donald Miller, *Blue Like Jazz* (Nashville: Thomas Nelson, Inc., 2003).
[4] 2 Corinthians 6.16
[5] Matthew 26.8
[6] Ecclesiastes 9.11
[7] Romans 8.28
[8] Fiona Apple, "Extraordinary Machine," *Extraordinary Machine* (Epic Records, 2005).

Chapter Two – Transformation: A Primal Reality
[1] Romans 12.2
[2] M. Robert Mulholland, Jr., *Invitation to a Journey* (IL:InterVarsity Press, 1993) 23.
[3] Philippians 1.6
[4] *Life As a House* (Winkler Films, 2001).
[5] 2 Corinthians 4.16
[6] Nehemiah 4.10
[7] Nehemiah 4.2
[8] Exodus 34.29–35
[9] Exodus 26.31–32
[10] Matthew 27.50–51
[11] C. S. Lewis, *Til We Have Faces* (United States:Harcourt, Inc, 1956) 292–294.

[12] Gregory Maguire, *Mirror Mirror* (NY: ReganBooks, 2003) 52.

[13] Brother Lawrence & Frank Laubach, *Practicing His Presence* (Sargent, Georgia: SeedSowers Publishing House, 1973) 19.

Chapter Three – Sanctuary: The Blueprints of Transformation

[1] 1 Corinthians 3.16

[2] Andrew Cross, *Theology, Mystery and an Old Riddle* (http://www.goodseed.com/learning/article/theology-mystery-and-an-old-riddle).

[3] Beth Moore, *A Woman's Heart: God's Dwelling Place* (Nashville, TN: Lifeway Press, 1995).

[4] Leviticus 16.1–2; Hebrews 9.7

[5] Hebrews 3.1

[6] John 1.29

[7] Hebrews 10.20

[8] John 8.12

[9] Romans 3.25–26

[10] John 6.35

[11] Exodus 15.17

[12] Exodus 25.8

[13] 1 Chronicles 28.10

[14] Exodus 35.30–40.33

[15] Acts 17.24

[16] Brother Lawrence & Frank Laubach, *Practicing His Presence* (Sargent, Georgia: SeedSowers Publishing House, 1973) 15.

[17] Exodus 40.9–15

[18] Ezekiel 5.11–12

[19] Hebrews 8.1–2

[20] Hebrews 8.5

[21] Psalm 102.19

[22] Ephesians 2.19–22

[23] 1 Corinthians 3.16

[24] 2 Chronicles 5–7.2

[25] Exodus 40.34–38

[26] Psalm 73.1–16

[27] *Turn Your Eyes Upon Jesus*, Helen H. Limmel.

[28] Psalm 20.2

[29] John 1.14

[30] 1 Peter 1.15–16

[31] John W. Thompson, Randy Scruggs, *Lord Prepare Me* (Whole Armor Publishing Co. 1982).

[32] Luke 9.8–32

Chapter Four – Clean Sweep: Keep, Toss or Sell
[1] *The Lion King* (Walt Disney Pictures, 1984).

[2] *Clean Sweep* (TLC).

[3] Jennifer Kennedy Dean, *He Restores My Soul* (Nashville, TN: Broadman and Holman Publishers, 1999) 69.

[4] Revelation 3.20

[5] Hebrews 3.13

[6] Galatians 2.20; Colossians 3.5

[7] Ezekiel 36.26

[8] Anne Lamott, *Bird by Bird* (United States: Anchor Books, 1995) 167.

[9] Arnold J. Toynbee, *A Study of History* (Oxford University Press, 1934), Vol. VI, pp. 169–175.

[10] Barlow Girl, "Surrender," *BarlowGirl* (Word Entertainment LLC, 2004.

Chapter Five – Falling Apart: Between Invitation and Healing
[1] Daniel 9.17

[2] Matthew 24.1

[3] Some interpret Matthew 24 to be a prophecy of the end times rather than the destruction of the Jerusalem temple in AD 70. Either way, this chapter describes a time of great transition and works as a metaphor for personal deconstruction.

[4] About 40 years after Jesus' death, the temple was permanently destroyed by the Romans, along with all the sacred elements of worship and sacrifice. The outer walls still stand and although renovation efforts have been attempted, none have been successful.

[5] Philippians 4.13

[6] David Schnarch, Ph.D. *Passionate Marriage* (NY: Henry Holt and Company, LLC, 1997) 351.

[7] 1 John 4.4

[8] Oswald Chambers, *My Utmost for His Highest* (Oswald Chambers Publications Assn., Ltd., 1963) December 30.

[9] Soren Kierkegaard, Albert B. Anderson, Edited by Reidar Thomte, *The Concept of Anxiety: Kierkegaard's Writings Volume 8* (Princeton, NJ: Princeton University Press, 1981), 155. Although Kierkegaard's con-

cern is the relationship of anxiety to inherited sin, his definition of anxiety is relevant to other discussions on this persistently observable state of man. Kierkegaard says that anxiety is based on the deep fear of all mankind that we are alone in this universe. He likens the dawning of the sense of infinity to the dizziness one might feel when peering into a "yawning abyss." He claims that it is not the reality of that abyss but the recognition of it which creates anxiety, for, until one looks into it, they are not dizzy. Thus it is the tension of our inate insecurity along with the contemplation of the possibilities of the infinite (freedom) which causes the experience we call anxiety. This disquiet causes us to steady ourselves by holding onto the finite (p. 61). The problem this creates is further addressed in Chapter Nine: The Total Perspective Vortex.

[10] *Ibid.*, Introduction xvii.

[11] E. Allison Peers, *Dark Night of the Soul: A Masterpiece in the Literature of Mysticism by St. John of the Cross* (New York, NY: Doubleday, 1990).

[12] Hebrews 12.18–28

[13] Exodus 19.16–18

[14] Nichole Nordeman, "Live," *Brave* (Sparrow Records, 2005).

[15] Hebrews 4.12

[16] Psalm 41.9

[17] William Shakespeare, *Julius Caesar,* Act 3, scene 2, 181–186.

[18] Leonard Cohen, "Anthem," *The Future* (Sony Music Entertainment, Inc., 1992).

[19] Emerson Hart, "Flying," *Cigarettes and Gasoline* (The Blue Note Label Group, 2007).

[20] Henri J.M. Nouwen, "From Resentment to Gratitude" as quoted in *Seeds of Hope,* Edited by Robert Durback (United States: Bantam Books, 1989), 79.

[21] Carl Jung, *"The Vision Seminars"* (Spring Publications, 1976) 206.

[22] Martin Luther, *Lectures on Galatians (1535)* in *Luther's Works,* editors Jaroslav Pelikan and Helmut T. Lehmann (St. Louis: Concordia; Philadelphia: Muhlenberg, 1955–1976). Vols. 26 and 27.

[23] Exodus 14.11–16

[24] John 14.6

[25] 1 Corinthians 15.16–19

[26] Oswald Chambers, *My Utmost for His Highest, April 9.*

[27] Shinedown, "45," *Leave a Whisper* (Atlantic Recording Corp., 2003).

[28] A phrase from Joseph Campbell's *The Hero of a Thousand Faces.*
[29] Isaiah 43.1–2

Chapter Six – Men Bring Stones
[1] Hosea 12.2–4
[2] Genesis 31.44–53
[3] *Shrek,* (Dreamworks, 2001).
[4] M. Robert Mulholland, Jr., *Invitation to a Journey,* 41.
[5] Psalm 119.11
[6] Romans 8.26
[7] Daniel 11.31
[8] "Temple of Jerusalem" Brittanica Online: http://www.britannica.com/EBchecked/topic/302895/Temple-of-Jerusalem#ref=ref27390.
[9] Genesis 28.16
[10] Genesis 28.20
[11] Leviticus 4.27–29
[12] Leviticus 1–7, specifically 7.37–38
[13] Numbers 5.12–31
[14] Numbers 5.15
[15] Numbers 5.31
[16] Jonah 1.1–16
[17] 2 Corinthians 4.11
[18] Exodus 3.10–4.12
[19] Judges 6.11–16
[20] Jeremiah 1.4–8
[21] Matthew 25.14–30, specifically verse 24
[22] Isaiah 61.3
[23] Joel 2.25
[24] Psalm 90.15
[25] Romans 8.24
[26] Luke 22.31–32
[27] Joseph Campbell, *The Hero With a Thousand Faces,* p. 17.
[28] Romans 4 and 5, esp. 4.22–25
[29] *The Solid Rock,* Edward Mote.
[30] Joseph Campbell, *The Power of Myth,* Vol. 1.
[31] Isaiah 61.1–4
[32] Psalm 127.1

Open Your Mind: Participating in the Building Process
Chapter Seven – Do-It-Yourself Detective Kit
[1] C.S. Lewis, *The Weight of Glory* (New York, NY: HarperCollins, 2001) 34.
[2] 1 Kings 8.37–40
[3] 2 Corinthians 13.5
[4] Christine Northurup, The Wisdom of Menopause (NY: Bantam Books, 2001) 55.
[5] *Ibid.*, p. 58.
[6] *Ibid.*, p. 62.
[7] John 16.7–8
[8] See Gary Chapman, *The Five Love Languages* (Chicago: Northfield Publishing, 1992, 1995, 2004).
[9] John 8.7
[10] John 8.36
[11] 2 Corinthians 2.7
[12] David Schnarch, M.D. *Passionate Marriage*, p. 18.
[13] *Ibid.*, p 337.
[14] James 1.14
[15] Gregory Maguire, *Mirror Mirror*, p. 2.
[16] Orson Scott Card, *Ender's Game* (New York, NY: Tom Doherty Associates, LLC, 1994).
[17] Matthew 26.39
[18] Genesis 32.24–30; *cf.* Hosea 12.4
[19] Job 3–31
[20] William P. Young, *The Shack* (CA: Windblown Media, 2007) 189.
[21] George K. Chesteron, *On Running After One's Hat, All Things Considered, 1908.*
[22] John 10.10
[23] Jeremiah 2.13

Chapter Eight – Defining Moments
[1] Emerson Hart, *Ordinary*/Album: Cigarettes and Gasoline (Blue Note Label, 2007).
[2] *Daffy Duck's Quackbusters* (Warner Bros. Pictures, 1988).
[3] John 10.18
[4] Elie Wiesel, *Night* (New York, NY: Hill and Wang, 1958) 5.
[5] Philippians 4.7
[6] C.S. Lewis, *The Great Divorce: A Dream* (United States: HarperCol-

lins, 2001) 71–72.

[7] *Ibid.*, p. 100.

[8] Psalm 106.9–15

[9] Byron Katie, *Loving What Is* (New York: Harmony Books, 2002).

[10] *24*, Television series, Fox Broadcasting Co.

[11] Colossians 3.1

[12] Philippians 4.6–8

[13] Genesis 26.24; Jeremiah 46.28

[14] John H. Sammis, *Trust and Obey* in Hymns Old and New (Chicago, Illinois: Fleming H. Revell Company, 1887).

[15] Galatians 5.4

[16] John 14.15

[17] Ephesians 2.8

[18] 2 Corinthians 3.4–5

[19] 2 Timothy 4.7

[20] Isaiah 64.6

[21] Luke 17.9–10

[22] M. Robert Mulholland, Jr., *Invitaiton to a Journey*, p. 22.

[23] Madeleine L'Engle, *Walking on Water* (New York: North Point Press), 162.

[24] Galatians 5.22–23

[25] 1 Chronicles 4.10

[26] Oswald Chambers, *My Utmost for His Highest*, October 30.

[27] Matthew 21.13

[28] Jeremiah 17.9

[29] Hosea 10.13

[30] Jeremiah 10.23

[31] Richard Wilbur, *"Two Voices in the Meadow"* from *Advice to a Prophet and Other Poems* in *Collected Poems 1943-2004* (United States: Harcourt, Inc., 2006) 257.

Open Your Heart: Enjoying the House

Chapter Nine – Total Perspective Vortex: You Are Here

[1] Marilynne Robinson, *Gilead* (NY: Farrar, Straus and Giroux, 2004) 245–246.

[2] Matthew 26.11

[3] Luke 6.39

[4] Revelation 21.4

[5] Psalm 56.8

[6] Hebrews 3.1; 12.3

[7] Hebrews 2.7

[8] Hebrews 2.9

[9] John 14.6

[10] Hebrews 2.10

[11] Hebrews 2.13–18

[12] Hebrews 3.1–6

[13] Psalm 30.5

[14] Nehemiah 8.10

[15] 2 Corinthians 12.9

[16] Douglas Adams, *The Hitchhiker's Guide to the Universe* (NY: Harmony Books, 1979).

[17] Douglas Adams, *The Restaurant at the End of the Universe* (United States: Del Rey Books, 2005) 76–77.

[18] Professor Jerry Root, Ph.D., Wheaton College, Video: *Be Still* (Beverly Hills, California: Twentieth Century Fox Home Entertainment, 2006).

[19] Romans 5.8

[20] Philippians 3.10

[21] Stephen King, *Misery* (NY: Signet, 1988).

[22] Romans 8.17

[23] Romans 8.18

[24] Romans 8.19–22

[25] Romans 8.28

[26] Romans 8.29

[27] 2 Timothy 1.1

[28] 2 Timothy 1.9

[29] 2 Timothy 1.13

[30] Romans 8.35, NLT

[31] Romans 5.5

[32] 1 John 4.21

[33] Matthew 17.20

[34] John 11.1–3

[35] 1 John 4.18

[36] Soren Kierkegaard, *Fear and Trembling* (United States: Cambridge Univesity Press, 2006) 29.

[37] *WordNet® 3.0*. Princeton University. 17 May. 2008. <Dictionary.com: http://dictionary.reference.com/browse/resignation>.

[38] Derek Redmon, Visa commercial, You Tube: http://www.youtube.com/watch?v=VO8b-zIKixM.

[39] 100 Greatest Tearjerkers, http://www.channel4.com/film/newsfeatures/microsites/T/tearjerkers/results/80-71.html. Number 77.

[40] Leonard Cohen, "Hallelujah," *The Essential Leonard Cohen* (Sony BMG Music Entertainment, 2002).

[41] 1 Corinthians 13.8

[42] Genesis 32.24–30

[43] Genesis 32.30

[44] Nathan Ward, *The Growth of the Seed* (Chillicothe: DeWard Publishing Company, 2007), 330.

[45] William Blake, "The Little Black Boy" from *Songs of Innocence and Experience* (Oxford: Oxford University Press, 1977).

Epilogue: The Face of the Father

[1] Job 1

[2] Job 2.8

[3] Job 2.9

[4] Job 3.25–26

[5] Job 16.20

[6] Job 19.2

[7] Job 16.2

[8] Job 32.32

[9] Job 32.21

[10] Job 40.4

[11] Job 42.3–6

[12] Joseph Campbell, *The Hero With a Thousand Faces*, 148.

[13] *Ibid.*, p. 148.

[14] *Ibid.*, p. 147.

[15] Harold Brodkey, "Manipulations." *Ms* 4.4 (1975): 74–76, 92–93, 116.

Want More?

Contact Gina Calvert with your questions and comments, to schedule a speaking engagement, or to make purchases and bulk orders of this book:

Gina Calvert
P.O. Box 1521
Coppell, TX 75019

calvertgina@yahoo.com
ginacalvert.blogspot.com
www.fromgraveltoglory.com

ALSO FROM DEWARD PUBLISHING:

The Growth of the Seed: Notes on the Book of Genesis (Nathan Ward)
A study of the book of Genesis that emphasizes two primary themes: the development of the Messianic line and the growing enmity between the righteous and the wicked. In addition, it provides detailed comments on the text and short essays on several subjects that are suggested in, yet peripheral to, Genesis. 540 pages.

The Man of Galilee (Atticus G. Haygood)
An apologetic for the deity of Christ using Jesus Himself as presented by the gospel records as its chief evidence. This is a reprint of the 1963 edition. The Man of Galilee was originally published in 1889. 108 pages.

Beneath the Cross: Essays and Reflections on the Lord's Supper
(Jady S. Copeland and Nathan Ward, editors)
The Lord's Supper is rich with meaning supplied by Old Testament foreshadowing and New Testament teaching. Explore the depths of symbolism and meaning found in the last hours of the Lord's life in *Beneath the Cross*. Filled with short essays by preachers, scholars, and other Christians, this book is an excellent tool for preparing meaningful Lord's Supper thoughts—or simply for personal study and meditation. 336 pages.

Churches of the New Testament (Ethan R. Longhenry)
A study designed to investigate every local congregation concerning which the Bible provides some information: it considers the geography and history of each city, whatever is known about the beginnings of the church in the city, and an analysis of the church based upon what is revealed in the New Testament. 150 pages.

The Big Picture of the Bible (Kenneth W. Craig)
In this short book, the author summarizes the central theme of the Bible in a simple, yet comprehensive approach. Evangelists across the world have used this presentation to convert countless souls to the discipleship of Jesus Christ. Bulk discounts will be available, as will special pricing for congregational orders. 48 pages. Full color illustrations.

*For cover art, sample pages, or information about ordering these books call **800.300.9778** or visit our website at **www.dewardpublishing.com**.*

DEWARD
PUBLISHING COMPANY

Printed in the United States
135973LV00002B/24/P